# SHORT CUTS

INTRODUCTIONS TO FILM STUDIES

# OTHER TITLES IN THE SHORT CUTS SERIES

THE HORROR GENRE: FROM BEELZEBUB TO BLAIR WITCH
Paul Wells

THE STAR SYSTEM: HOLLYWOOD'S PRODUCTION OF POPULAR IDENTITIES
Paul McDonald

SCIENCE FICTION CINEMA: FROM OUTERSPACE TO CYBERSPACE
Geoff King and Tanya Krzywinska

EARLY SOVIET CINEMA: INNOVATION, IDEOLOGY AND PROPAGANDA
David Gillespie

READING HOLLYWOOD: SPACES AND MEANINGS IN AMERICAN FILM
Deborah Thomas

DISASTER MOVIES: THE CINEMA OF CATASTROPHE
Stephen Keane

THE WESTERN GENRE: FROM LORDSBURG TO BIG WHISKEY
John Saunders

PSYCHOANALYSIS AND CINEMA: THE PLAY OF SHADOWS
Vicky Lebeau

COSTUME AND CINEMA: DRESS CODES IN POPULAR FILM
Sarah Street

MISE-EN-SCÈNE: FILM STYLE AND INTERPRETATION
John Gibbs

NEW CHINESE CINEMA: CHALLENGING REPRESENTATIONS
Sheila Cornelius with Ian Haydn Smith

SCENARIO: THE CRAFT OF SCREENWRITING
Tudor Gates

ANIMATION: GENRE AND AUTHORSHIP
Paul Wells

WOMEN'S CINEMA: THE CONTESTED SCREEN
Alison Butler

BRITISH SOCIAL REALISM: FROM DOCUMENTARY TO BRIT GRIT
Samantha Lay

# FILM EDITING

## THE ART OF THE EXPRESSIVE

### VALERIE ORPEN

**WALLFLOWER**

LONDON and NEW YORK

A Wallflower Paperback

First published in Great Britain in 2003 by Wallflower Press, 5 Pond Street, London NW3 2PN
www.wallflowerpress.co.uk

A catalogue record for this book is available from the British Library

ISBN 1 903364 53 1

Book Design by Rob Bowden Design

Printed in Great Britain by Antony Rowe Ltd, Chippenham, Wiltshire

# CONTENTS

## ACKNOWLEDGEMENTS

This book began its life as a doctoral thesis and so my first thanks go to my supervisor, V.F. Perkins, whose constructive criticism was hugely stimulating, inspiring and helpful, as well as to all the staff in the Film and Television Studies Department at the University of Warwick for their help and feedback, and to the British Academy for their financial assistance. My research was greatly facilitated by the librarians at the University of Warwick library, the University College London library and the British Film Institute library.

I am also grateful to Adrian Armstrong, Catherine Constable, Greg Crosbie, Ed Gallafent, John Gibbs, Heather Laing, Rachel Moseley, John Orpen, Alastair Phillips, Fiona Ponikwer, Luke Scofield, Murray Smith and Ginette Vincendeau for providing feedback, encouragement and support, as well as drawing my attention to or providing relevant books, articles, videotapes and other material.

*In memory of my mother, Nicole (1931–1995). For my father, John.*

# INTRODUCTION:   EDITING – DOING THE 'WASHING UP'

*What is editing?*

Editing straddles the line between art and craft, or as Mike Crisp puts it, 'it comes in a category somewhere between brain surgery at one extreme and tiling the bathroom at the other' (1996: 79). Similarly, the French director Claude Chabrol has compared editing to doing the washing-up: 'Scriptwriting is like cooking. Shooting, the part I enjoy most, is like eating. Editing therefore is, well, the washing-up' (quoted in Crawley 1991: 104). However, the Soviet film-makers of the 1920s, such as Vsevolod Pudovkin, Sergei Eisenstein and Lev Kuleshov, considered editing to be the creative force of film and the foundation of film art.

The editing process can be divided into three stages: the selection of takes and their length; the arrangement and timing of shots, scenes and sequences; and their combination with the soundtrack. Editing is primarily (though not exclusively) a connective process, that is, the joining of shots to form a whole. The film editor Walter Murch has noted that the process has created interesting linguistic nuances: 'In the States, film is "cut", which puts the emphasis on *separation*. In Australia (and in Great Britain), film is "joined" [or "spliced"] with the emphasis on *bringing together*' (1995: 5). The differences between French and English are even more telling: the French use the verb 'raccorder' meaning literally 'to join'. In English, there is a distinction between editing and *montage** whereas in

––––––––

* terms indicated with an asterisk throughout the book are defined in the Glossary

1

French, both terms are conflated into one, 'le montage' (which is regularly mistranslated). Conversely, the French use the term 'découpage' to describe the last stage of scriptwriting but also the film's structure after the final cut. There is no English translation for this latter meaning, although 'découpage classique' is generally translated as *continuity editing\**, hinting at the importance of the script.[1] Noël Burch devotes two influential chapters to the principles of editing in his celebrated *Theory of Film Practice* (1973). The first chapter, entitled 'Spatial and Temporal Articulations', begins with a useful analysis of film terminology, or more precisely, the explanation of the French term 'découpage' that he has described elsewhere as 'the underlying structure of the *finished* film' (1969: 4). According to Burch, an awareness of this meaning helps to conceptualise film as a convergence of the spatial fragments of the shooting process with the temporal fragments established in the editing. In other words, 'découpage' as a structural concept helps to place editing in a much broader context.

In *On the History of Film Style*, David Bordwell has remarked that the term 'découpage' was adopted by the French new critics in the 1950s and 1960s: 'In postwar years, French critics often identified silent-film editing with montage and sound-film cutting with découpage' (1997: 52). So, from the outset, 'découpage' incorporates sound into its scope, presumably because sound can smooth over the possible disjuncture of editing. Despite its emphasis on the *cut\** (from *découper*, 'to cut up'), 'découpage', unlike 'editing', suggests that there is a very strong link between the shooting stage and post-production. In other words, the French term is more auteurist since, from the outset, the director is expected to exert some influence over the editing stage, even if s/he does not physically take part in it.

This interesting semantic field offers different approaches: 'cutting' and 'editing' suggest pruning, curtailing, rejecting, removing, while 'joining' conjures up the notion of adding and accreting, and 'découpage' broadens the import of editing and hints at its overarching design. These contrasting approaches reflect different aesthetics (and possibly also national differences): the whole versus fragmentation.

There are two principal ways of considering editing: either as connective or as expressive. Editing can be predominantly connective, or may appear so but in fact be subtly expressive. Editing may express or connect 'invisibly' or seamlessly, but it may also be graphically, temporally, spatially and/or rhythmically ostentatious. Of course, invisibility is relative and depends on a 'norm' which is taken to be classical continuity editing.

It is the expressive dimensions of film editing which interest us here, not the connective aspect, which has been studied either in filmmakers'/editors' handbooks or by the cognitive school of film scholarship. Of course, the two forms of editing often merge as we shall see, for instance, in films such as *A bout de souffle* (1959): the rules of continuity are violated, which leads to an expressivity of its own.

It soon transpires from the literature that editing as an expressive technique is largely taken for granted. We all know that it is expressive, but it is more difficult, uncomfortable even, to explain why and how. The expressiveness of lighting, camera movements, colour, sound and so forth has been explored to a large extent. Editing is far more elusive. Editing can be equated with movement but unlike camera movement or movement within the frame, it is difficult to pin down, to freeze, to control. As it is, the medium of film is lengthy to describe verbally, but describing editing seems even more difficult since its crucial element, time, is particularly arduous to quantify. In fact, Noël Burch uses a word which is almost synaesthetic, he calls the plastic aspect of editing 'intangible' (1973: 46).

## Does editing exist?

Or rather, is it possible to discuss editing? This question is not as facetious as it may seem. We know that editing exists even if it is often seamless: all films shot on 35mm film and over ten minutes long have to contain cuts, since a roll of film lasts only ten minutes. However, strictly speaking, editing exists only *in relation to*, as a *counterpart to*, the shot. In other words, it is impossible to isolate editing, to analyse the cuts *per se*, that thin line, or 'switching', that demarcates one shot from another. The upshot of this is both frustration and loss of interest: the study of editing seems elusive and not really desirable given that one must ultimately revert to the shot anyway, which leads to a sort of vicious circle.

In his second chapter, 'Editing as a Plastic Art' in *The Theory of Film Practice*, Burch raises the issue of subliminal perception, a stumbling block in the study of editing. He uses an example from *La Notte* (1960): two discontinuous shots of a door being kicked shut and swinging open again are, according to Burch, 're-established' as a continuous movement in the spectator's mind. Though not passive or repressed as psychoanalysts would have us believe, spectators are not always conscious of cuts and instinctively 'fill in the gaps'. This subliminal aspect of film viewing tends to constitute an obstacle for the film scholar. If a cut (or even a shot) was not noticed by the audience, should we take this to mean that the editing was 'bad' (in the sense that it did not reach its goal) or that it was *intended* to pass unnoticed? In addition, we are often faced with the paradox that many effective cuts are effective precisely *because* they are not noticeable. Moreover, we are faced with a problem of limited knowledge: we do not know the extent of the coverage, namely the material that was shot, and what the editor discarded. Did the editing 'save' the film, or was there minimal coverage (as in an Alfred Hitchcock film, where superfluous takes were rare) which limited the editor's choices?

In effect, this book will appear to spend far more time poring over the content of shots than the actual cuts. Shots may seem irrelevant, but as Jean-Luc Godard famously asserted in his essay on editing in *Cahiers du Cinéma* (December 1956), 'Montage, mon beau souci', 'to speak of directing is automatically to speak, yet and again, of editing' (quoted in Mussman 1968: 48). And vice versa. Except that in many cases, in film theory and criticism, the two are divorced.

*Why study editing in the sound film?*

This book concentrates on editing in the sound film, although it occasionally also needs to refer to silent cinema. It is true that, on a practical and visual level, the principal features of film editing have not changed significantly since its 'invention' at the turn of the century. There has been technological progress, for example the Moviola in 1924 (Villain 1991: 38), then the KEM or Steenbeck in the 1960s and now the non-linear systems (AVID, Lightworks). Nevertheless, there is no doubt that the conflation of sound and image editing has not only changed the way editing makes meaning but also expresses ideas and emotions beyond what appears on the screen. Here are two examples:

- I recently watched Howard Hawks' 1939 comedy *His Girl Friday* again, though in unorthodox viewing conditions, namely on television and with the sound muted. I was struck by how *few* cuts there are, yet because the dialogue is delivered at breakneck speed, the film gives the impression of being rapidly cut. In other words, a consideration of sound soon renders obsolete and fallacious certain arguments articulated by silent cinema theorists regarding rhythm and pace.
- Sound can sometimes contradict image editing. Consider the mythical Kuleshov effect where the same shot of the actor Ivan Mosjoukine bearing a neutral facial expression is juxtaposed with shots of a plate of soup, a child playing and a woman in a coffin. The audience of the experiment was apparently touched by the last juxtaposition and thought the actor's expression was one of deep sorrow. But let us suppose that a lilting, upbeat tune had been played over them; how would the audience have reacted then?

Non-diegetic music can either reinforce the meaning of image editing or contradict it. For instance, in the horror or thriller genre, a series of ever-approaching point-of-view shots (where the subject's identity is concealed) intimate a threat, especially if they are accompanied by ominous music or the absence of music, but what would happen if the music was buoyant and reassuring?

Most editing is taken to mean visual editing. While it is not my purpose to examine the complex technicalities of sound editing, all my analyses will take into account the nature of the soundtrack, be it 'dead' (silent), or dominated by speech (dialogue, monologue, voice-over, and so on) or sound-effects or music (diegetic and non-diegetic). We hear a film as much as we see it, and sound and image are not always synchronous. Furthermore, there can be expressive discrepancies between visual and aural distance and balance. If, as Ingmar Bergman once observed, 'no

other form of art has as much in common with the cinema as has music'
(quoted in Bettetini 1973: 106), then what happens when the visual 'music'
of a film is complicated by acoustic music?

While reading the scholarship on editing, I discovered an almost
contemptuous attitude towards editing in the sound film mainly because
sound has been perceived as limiting the editor's freedom. While it is
true that editing was subservient to the dialogue (and the *mise-en-scène*
deferred to the strategic placing of microphones) in the early days of
sound, these impediments were soon circumvented. Yet some critics still
insist that the art of editing is irrecoverably lost. It is only dialogue that
impedes the editor, but visual and aural permutations are nevertheless
numerous. One may be forgiven for thinking that editing after 1927 is
simply not worth writing about, except perhaps to make a small foray into
the connective properties of continuity editing or to praise the long-take
style of the 1940s. Film histories are quite remarkable in this respect:
if editing appears in the index at all, it is linked to merely two names:
D.W. Griffith and Sergei Eisenstein, or 'Soviet Montage'.[2] But more often
than not, editing is not listed, although 'montage' sometimes appears.[3]
Finally, the *Oxford History of World Cinema* (Nowell-Smith 1996) does not
even contain the words 'editing' or 'montage' in the index or the table of
contents. A notable exception is David Cook's *A History of Narrative Film*
(1996), which discusses editing and its various permutations at length.

Finally, Don Fairservice, a film editor who has taught in British film
schools, has written a very welcome and comprehensive book on editing.
*Film Editing: History, Theory and Practice* (2001) is not a technical handbook and, so the jacket informs us, purports to explain 'not only the "how"
but also the "why" of this pivotal filmmaking activity'. This sounds very
promising, but Fairservice, like many other writers, has chosen to focus
primarily on the first 35 years of cinema history, 'largely because, in terms
of structural analysis, it does seem to be the most neglected' (2001: 1). Yet,
in terms of the analysis of film editing, sound editing, particularly in the
continuity system, seems to be far more neglected.

Broadly speaking, the study of the expressiveness of film editing has
been polarised: montage theory (championed by Eisenstein) on the one
hand, deep focus editing (extolled by André Bazin) on the other. Both theo-

ries attempt to demonstrate that one editing style is 'better' or more effective than the other, for ideological purposes – communist for Eisenstein, Catholic for Bazin. For Eisenstein, montage could create meaning not immediately evident in the shots themselves, and thus highlight social inequalities. For Bazin, avoidance of editing presented the world as God had created it, with the least possible human intervention. More recent film writing tends to ignore editing in favour of *mise-en-scène* or narrative structure. I am concerned not so much with the causes of this neglect as with the need to redress the balance.

## Rhetoric: editing and the audience

In interviews with film editors, or in editing handbooks, the word 'audience' recurs with remarkable frequency. In an interview, Robert Wise – who was an editor, most notably on *Citizen Kane* (1941), before turning to direction – asserted that 'as the editor, you're the audience' (*Film Comment*, March–April 1977: 21). Often, the director can also 'be' the audience. When Martin Scorsese edits his films with Thelma Schoonmaker, he assumes the role of the audience by using the first person plural, 'we', when questioning a cut's validity and meaning (see Schiff 1996).

Given that film is an industry as well as an art and must therefore prove financially viable, every stage of film-making has to consider, sometimes even pander to, the audience. Editing, however, seems to reveal an even greater awareness of the audience, probably because making changes to the editing is the last resort (bar reshooting certain scenes) if a film does not appeal to a (preview) audience. Editing can 'save' or maim a film (*La Règle du jeu*, 1939, and *The Magnificent Ambersons*, 1942, are celebrated examples of maimed films). 'Directors' cuts' have become increasingly popular (Francis Ford Coppola's *Apocalypse Now Redux*, 1979/2001; Ridley Scott's *Blade Runner*, 1982), probably because the editing controlled by the director is generally perceived as being the more felicitous version. Whereas the shooting is fairly immutable, being subservient to actor, crew and location availability, the editing stage is never finished; it can be rejigged and reshuffled *ad infinitum*, provided there is sufficient time and money available. The basic questions are: will the audience understand the action (despite the *180° line** being crossed, for example)? Will they take it all in (is this complex shot held long enough to be absorbed)? Will the audience respond in the way that is expected of them? On the strength of this patent attentiveness to the audience, which goes towards explaining cultural and national differences in editing styles, we might think of the arsenal of editing devices as strongly rhetorical.

'Rhetoric' is not a very user-friendly word. It carries overtones of political sophistry and bombast through its association with oratory. Alternatively, it suggests a preoccupation with style over content. Since its invention, allegedly by Empedocles (see Ricœur 1978), in the early fifth century BC, it has outgrown its original concern with persuasive public speaking or direct verbal communication and now lends itself to written and visual communication as well (see Lanham 1991). The belief in the orator's moral obligation has also been abandoned; in fact we now tend to take the Platonic view that rhetoric is largely concerned with manipulation and deception, which is neither accurate nor relevant here.

According to Cicero, the orator had three 'offices' or main functions: to teach, to please and to move. These offices could be applied equally well to editing. In its broader sense, namely the art of using language effectively, not simply to persuade but also to emphasise and influence, freed of its derogatory connotations, rhetoric is relevant to the cinema and editing in particular. Film does admittedly appear to function like language, with its own set of (mutable) conventions, although as semiotics revealed, parallels between shots and words, or shots and morphemes (words) or phonemes (sounds that make up words), scenes and sentences, and sequences and paragraphs are by no means watertight. Film can have rhetorical figures in a similar way to literature, namely arrangements of shots (for example repetition, gradually shorter takes, and so on) to achieve a particular emphasis which does not alter the meaning of single shots but colours the meaning of the scene, the sequence or the entire film.

But what sort of 'figures' are we talking about here? There are hundreds, if not thousands, of rhetorical figures in speech and literature. Some figures have already been incorporated into film theory and criticism, mainly as categories of film semiology, such as the trope, which is usually applied to *mise-en-scène* (James Monaco (1981) sees the swish pan as a trope, for example), the symbol, the metonymy, the synecdoche, and the metaphor. All these figures are associated with *mise-en-scène* rather than editing, although one figure, the ellipsis, is often mentioned in relation to editing. However, N. Roy Clifton points out that given the nature of film, which is composed of frames joined together and projected one after the other, 'it cannot escape a figurative character since every frame and every piece must in some degree be coloured in meaning by all the frames or pieces projected before it' (1983: 205). Clifton is speaking more specifically of the nature of film *editing* here. In other words, the study of a rhetoric of film is almost always compelled to refer to editing at some point.

This said, whereas rhetoric (extant as an art and a discipline until the nineteenth century) is perceived as being based on fairly fixed rules, editing does not really have rules that are set in stone. There are prescriptive handbooks (for example, Roy Thompson's *Grammar of the Edit* (1993)) but the general consensus is that if these rules were followed strictly, films would be somewhat predictable and dull. As Thompson concludes, 'creativity overrules grammar' (1993: 72). In *Theory of Film Practice*, Noël Burch sets about cataloguing all the possible spatial and temporal articulations between consecutive shots (15 in total). While this is very useful as a checklist, it does not lead to any ground-breaking conclusion but merely designates 'rules' which were previously hazy or tacit. However, this raises the question of generality and specificity, one of the stumbling blocks to the study of editing. If, as many editors claim, there are no real 'rules', if every film has to be approached with a fresh vision, does this imply that the study of editing is also different with every film? The rules that exist are primarily aesthetic and privilege coherence. But editing, like anything else, is subject to fads and fashions: Soviet montage, long takes, 'bad' editing of the 1960s, MTV-style editing and so on, which are so many gambles with audience response.

The word 'emotion' recurs often in the context of editing. Walter Murch's first criteria for an ideal cut are 'emotion', then 'story' and finally 'rhythm', which are all connected (1995: 20). This insistence on emotion challenges the impression that editing is a pragmatic and rational craft. Or rather, it is rational in as much as it favours emotion to attain a specific end: to make the audience react. This seems at odds with the intellectual slant of rhetoric, especially since many editors consider their craft to be primarily instinctive, intuitive and emotional, but also disciplined and ordered. Therefore, if one is to use the framework of rhetoric, it should be with the emphasis on the emotional rather than the moral or the aesthetic, even though all three tend to overlap to a certain extent. It should also be remembered that another important motivation to make a cut is to keep the audience interested, and interest is often the result of emotion. This constitutes the second 'office' of rhetoric: to please.

I therefore intend to use rhetoric in its broader sense, namely the art of using editing to persuade, influence or please. But, by persuade, I mean to draw the spectator into the world and process of the film, rather than to sway his or her moral beliefs. I intend to show that, rather than a multitude of figures as in the rhetoric of literature, two figures stand out in particular in the rhetoric of editing: repetition and alternation.

*Existing literature on editing*

The existing literature on editing can be divided into three categories: textbooks or general studies on film, either solely on editing or books with a section on editing; editors' handbooks; and interviews with film editors, which include autobiographies, transcripts of lectures, essays, anthologies of interviews and individual interviews in periodicals. Very often, the critical scholarship on individual films can prove more useful than works on editing in general.

Textbooks, such as David Bordwell and Kristin Thompson's *Film Art: An Introduction*, first published in 1979, provide clear definitions of editing, but are more concerned with the connective properties of editing. Chapter seven of *Film Art* is devoted to editing, clearly defining what constitutes continuity editing, its alternatives and the general principles of editing. The authors are evidently concerned with narrative coherence rather than expressiveness, especially in terms of time and space. In the introduction to the chapter, the authors write that editing is a very powerful technique; however, the examples they provide are of celebrated montage sequences (the Odessa steps in *Battleship Potemkin* (1925), 'News on the March' in *Citizen Kane*, the shower scene in *Psycho* (1960), and so on) as if editing were only effective when it is memorable. This is worth reflecting on, for what strikes me as unique to editing is that it is usually impossible to remember correctly after viewing a film, no matter how many times one has seen it. It is possible to remember dialogue exactly to the word, or a facial expression, or a melody, or even a camera movement. But a fade? A discreet cut to a reverse-shot of a character reacting? One may recall the editing *style* of a whole film, but rarely the particulars. Bordwell and Thompson run through the nuts and bolts of editing – graphic, rhythmic, spatial and temporal relations between shots – but this is a textbook and must often be schematic. Typically, continuity editing is emphasised as a *system,* whose goal is to tell a story as coherently and as clearly as possible. Nowhere is it suggested that this system could also be individual. Bordwell and Thompson do not consider that some of the 'hiccups' in continuity that are mentioned (crossing the axis for example) could in fact be deliberate.

Editors' technical handbooks, which are aimed mainly at (tyro-)editors, are comprehensive and obligatory introductions to editing. Two fine examples are Dominique Villain's *Le Montage au cinéma* (1991), and *The Technique of Film Editing* by Karel Reisz and Gavin Millar (1996). Neither is simply practical, but also supplies a historical and theoretical framework. *Le Montage au cinéma* provides an alternative approach to Reisz and Millar, in so far as its angle is predominantly French and auteurist. Villain repeatedly stresses that it is the director who begets the editing, especially in France: 'In France, film-makers ... are responsible for their editing' thanks to a law passed in 1957 (1991: 12). She suggests that the notion of *auteur,* created by the New Wave critics, is intrinsically associated with the director's claim to a right over the editing of his or her film.

Villain also attempts to explain the overriding number of female film editors in the history of French editing. She draws an interesting analogy between the dominant spectator (female) and the editor, which partly explains why the few female editors in Hollywood during the classical era were supervising editors who worked in collaboration with the producers (predating test audiences). This analogy stems from Villain's assertion that one of the prerequisites to becoming a good editor is first and foremost to be a good, active spectator who can grasp the director's way of thinking immediately. Villain agrees with Jean-Luc Godard, who opposes 'masculine' direction to 'feminine' editing, because editing requires 'a certain sense of organisation, at once material and intellectual' (1991: 60). This does not explain, however, the overwhelming number of male editors in Hollywood, especially in the classical era.

A relatively recent phenomenon is the interview with the editor, and even anthologies of interviews with editors to which could also be added the editor autobiography.[4] Before the 1960s, editors were seldom invited to speak about their role and their art, although Margaret Booth was a notable exception (see Watts 1938). But since the 1960s, possibly as a reaction to auteurism, editors have been able to divulge the secrets of their craft. Editors are still 'invisible' (we rarely see them in documentaries on the making of films and they are not prominent guests at awards ceremonies) but they are recognised and well-documented production artists, and two major anthologies of interviews testify to their insight and their historical utility, whether artistic or technical.[5]

These works are interesting to read in their own right: they bring a mere name in the credits to life and, more importantly, hold invaluable information for aspiring or experienced editors. However, entertaining as they are, these interviews are largely concerned with the motivations behind editing rather than the end result. We are aware that a strong motivating factor in editing is amendment or abridgement. We also learn that in certain cases the choice of a take is very limited, or that a revolutionary style of cutting was the product of chance and accident. These interviews brim with anecdotes and factual information (for instance the time pressures on editors) but these are not relevant to the effect of the finished film. For even if one knows that the 'energy cuts' in *Bonnie and Clyde* (1967) were the result of accident, the effect on the viewer remains exactly the same. Editors sometimes mention expressiveness and separate it from background and motivation, but generally speaking, these interviews or biographies are very clearly aimed at a film industry readership rather than critics or theorists.

In this category, we could include one of the most concise and profound texts to have been written on editing, Godard's 1956 article. Godard was well-versed in editing before becoming a film-maker; indeed, the final sentence in the article makes it clear that he believed editing to be the best possible training in becoming a director. Most importantly,

Godard stresses the indivisible link between shooting and editing, which may seem obvious but is rarely articulated, at least in British and American scholarship. For Godard, good editing gives the impression that a film was directed, but outstanding editing gives the impression that no directing was needed at all! He argues that whereas shooting anticipates space, editing anticipates time, although the two are obviously connected: 'Cutting on a look is almost the definition of editing, its supreme ambition as well as its subjection to *mise-en-scène*' (1989: 79). This is supremely ironic, since Godard would subsequently jettison the convention of eye-line matches in *A bout de souffle*. But what this article reveals is that Godard was aware of the rules, only to break them later.

Finally, there exists a category that we might label 'peripheral', namely of articles or chapters that do not address editing directly but obliquely. Brian Henderson's (1976) essay on the long take is one such example. At first glance, Henderson's essay appears to be the negative image of texts on editing, but in fact he engages far more with editing than with *mise-en-scène*. It soon becomes apparent that the two poles (avoidance of cuts/abundance of cuts) are inseparable. The novelty of the article lies in Henderson's expression of an overlooked truism: between long takes, there are cuts, and what is more, not all long takes are *plans-séquence\**, that is, shots that last a whole sequence. Henderson jettisons the notion that the long take is an isolated phenomenon, and observes that length can only be determined *in contrast to* other take lengths in a sequence or film. He also points out that the combination of long take and cutting is ignored by both Eisensteinian montage theory and Bazinian long-take theory, and proposes to fill this unexplained void.

In some of his essays, Bazin will not admit the possibility of expressive editing relations within long-take sequences, for he believes that *mise-en-scène* cannot be expressive because it replicates temporal reality. Henderson's point is that, whether long take or montage, a choice is always made. Long takes can also be expressive in the timing of the inter- or intra-sequence cuts which can break the rhythm of the sequence. What is more, long takes are arguably more noticeable than standard continuity editing, especially if they are infrequent or anomalous in the film. However, Henderson ignores the combination of rhythm within the frame (movement of characters or camera) and without (the cuts). But he does articulate the importance of cuts as *transposition* of *mise-en-scène* and his analysis of dialogue sequences, though not very detailed, illustrates this aptly. In short, this essay opens up a host of questions. It also illustrates a strange phenomenon, namely that much pertinent writing on editing did not intend to address editing to begin with. In other words, peripheral reading can be more rewarding than core reading.

In short, there is a dearth of studies on editing, particularly in the sound film. Textbooks and technical guides abound, but they have their limitations. Interviews with editors can prove more useful, though they usually do not address the expressive dimensions of the end result of editing. Peripheral literature, on the other hand, can yield surprising insights.

This study is divided into three chapters which rely to a large extent on textual analysis. Chapter 1 addresses the neglected area of continuity editing and explores the possible shifts in conventions and expressiveness from classical Hollywood conventions to New Hollywood editing. Point-of-view editing is also examined and opens up a discussion of character identification. If continuity editing is the 'norm', how does art cinema or experimental cinema distance itself from, or even jettison, that yardstick? Chapter 2 will look at the ways in which art cinema has sought an alternative expressiveness via a different cutting style.

Finally, Chapter 3 will focus on the ways in which editing articulates not only a character's state of mind but also an actor's performance and even a star's image. Another reason why I am particularly interested in the sound film is because sound encouraged the star system to blossom. An interest in sound editing thus comes into play with dialogue and the importance of many stars' distinctive voices.

By necessity, this book cannot be entirely comprehensive in its coverage of all types of editing, or all possible temporal/spatial editing combinations. Rather, its aim is to examine specific instances of expressive editing through a select number of case studies. I have chosen to analyse in depth the editing in three films in particular. The criteria I used in my selection was that these films needed to be reasonably well known and exemplars of a certain editing style. Another criterion was simply that I had to like and admire these films sufficiently for them to sustain repeated viewings. To get as much out of this book as possible, readers will need to be familiar with these three films, or better still, have them available on video or DVD.

A glossary can be found at the end of the book, providing definitions for editing terms along with a comprehensive bibliography of relevant literature and a filmography of all films discussed.

# 1    CONTINUITY EDITING IN HOLLYWOOD

Historically speaking, continuity editing has often been equated with Hollywood cinema, when in fact all Western national cinemas, particularly commercial or popular, rely on it to a large extent. Non-Hollywood and non-Western cinema, such as Japanese classical cinema, used different conventions which did not consider the 180° demarcation line as problematic for spatial comprehension.

How does one define continuity editing? It is commonly associated with the classical narrative system which enables a story to be narrated with the least possible disruption and disorientation to the viewer: 'The purpose of the system was *to tell a story* coherently and clearly, to map out the chain of characters' actions in an undistracting way' (Bordwell & Thompson 1986: 210). The narrative structure relies chiefly on enigma and resolution, a cause and effect relationship. The narrative must be propelled, there should be no flagging in the tempo and no digressions.

Since classical cinema's main purpose is supposedly to tell a story coherently and without distractions, it follows that continuity editing is not intended to be noticed, or rather, should never be obtrusive without good reason. It appears 'invisible' and 'seamless' and therein lies its strength and its staying-power. It must be emphasised, however, that these notions of 'visibility' and 'invisibility' are only relevant in the context of normal viewing conditions, namely during a first, uninterrupted projection in a cinema or on video/DVD. As soon as one begins to study a film, to examine it in detail, sequence by sequence, shot by shot, the visibility of even the most understated editing will become foregrounded.

How does this system achieve unobtrusiveness? Spatial continuity is respected thanks to certain strategies such as the *180 degree rule\**. The camera must not cross an imaginary line called variously 'the 180° line', 'the axis of action' or the 'centre line'. Should this happen, the spectator could feel disorientated. In fact, as we shall see, crossing the 180° line happens quite frequently and is not the result of incompetence, but is intentional. Similarly, sequences should begin with an establishing shot so that the spectator has a sense of where the sequence is set. In many cases, sequences will also contain re-establishing shots to reaffirm the spatial configuration.

Temporal continuity is conveyed through *eye-line matches\** and *matches on action\** which confirm that action or movement in two distinct shots was continuous or simultaneous. These matches are extremely effective because our eye and attention are sufficiently held by the action or gaze for the cut to be successfully camouflaged.

The origins of continuity editing coincide with the first newsreels: this system was a good way of unifying a series of disparate shots. In other words, seemingly disjointed events would appear to follow a narrative structure, disorder would become ordered and would acquire meaning. Continuity editing was subsequently adopted in fiction films to allow the narrative to flow coherently and to enhance narrative comprehension.

Continuity editing is still alive and well, and will probably never become extinct, although it is sometimes considered basic and over-simplistic. More importantly, it is perceived as entirely subservient to the narrative, and thus, not sufficiently creative or original (see Fairservice 2001). Finally, continuity editing is generally understood to follow a rigid set of rules. This, coupled with its unobtrusiveness, does not seem compatible with expressiveness.

This chapter will attempt to challenge this view by examining two examples of Hollywood styles of editing which both use a certain amount of continuity editing: an example from the heyday of classical Hollywood cinema, Alfred Hitchcock's *Rear Window* (1954) and a 'New Hollywood' film, Martin Scorsese's *Raging Bull* (1980), which blends continuity editing with art cinema editing styles as well as post-1960s editing. Both films testify to creativity and originality, although these are less immediately obvious in the former.

## A pre-cut picture?: Rear Window

*Rear Window* is one of Hitchcock's most famous and accomplished films. Based on a Cornell Woolrich short story, it deals with a news photographer, L.B. Jefferies, or 'Jeff' (James Stewart), who, confined to his Greenwich Village apartment with a broken leg, whiles away the time by observing his neighbours. He gradually suspects that one of them (played by Raymond Burr) has murdered his invalid wife. Jeff's detective friend Doyle (Wendell Corey) refuses to believe him, but using a lot of guesswork and some help from his fiancée Lisa Freemont (Grace Kelly) and his nurse Stella (Thelma Ritter), he is finally proved right, although this costs him a second broken leg in the wake of a struggle with the murderer.

Virtually the entire cast and crew of *Rear Window* get a mention in the production notes and reviews: Robert Burks, the cinematographer; Franz Waxman, the composer; John Michael Hayes, the scriptwriter; Edith Head, the costume designer; all the actors and the Master of Suspense himself. However, George Tomasini, the editor, is neglected. Yet this was Tomasini's first film with Hitchcock, the first of nine films, a collaboration which ended with Tomasini's death in 1964. He is one of the lesser-known film editors, yet his filmography is impressive: nine Hitchcock films over ten years, many of which are considered Hitchcock's best American movies: *To Catch a Thief* (1955); *The Man Who Knew Too Much* (1956); *The Wrong Man* (1957); *Vertigo* (1958); *North by Northwest* (1959); *Psycho* (1960); *The Birds* (1963); and *Marnie* (1964). He also worked with Billy Wilder (*Stalag 17*, 1953), John Huston (*The Misfits*, 1961) and Otto Preminger (*In Harm's Way*, 1965). However, Tomasini remains unmentioned and, even more astonishingly, so too does the editing in *Rear Window*. The former oversight can be explained by Hitchcock's claim to 'shoot a pre-cut picture' (Bouzereau 1993: 156), and since his scripts were worked out in advance, 'there [was] no opportunity for creative work on the part of the film editor' (La Valley 1972: 43). But the latter oversight is astonishing because *Rear Window* is, to a large extent, an editing-driven film.

In his famous interview with François Truffaut in 1967, Hitchcock defined *Rear Window* thus: 'It was a possibility of doing a purely cinematic film. You have an immobilised man looking out. That's one part of the film. The second part shows what he sees and the third part shows how he reacts' (quoted in Truffaut 1986: 319). In other words, between 'man looking', 'what man sees' and 'man's reaction', there have to be *cuts*.

*Rear Window* is unique for many reasons, not least for the insidious and almost uncanny way in which it can play tricks on one's memory. A lot of this 'trickery' has to do with the seamless editing and the conventions of point-of-view editing. Like the putative audience of the Kuleshov experiment, to which I shall return later, we think that we have seen something which in fact has not been shown. One of the main inaccuracies regarding *Rear Window* is the assertion that Jeff is in control, that the entire film is mediated through Jeff's point of view. True, many shots *are* from his point of view, but it is also important to note that Jeff's attention is frequently drawn to a character or an event across the courtyard by *somebody else*: both Lisa and Stella enjoin him to 'look!'. Finally, let us not forget that Jeff becomes the *object* of Thorwald's point of view at the film's climax.

*Rear Window* is clearly illustrative of film editing rhetoric. But when mentioning figures of rhetoric, it is important to bear in mind that these figures are *intended* to be noticed and understood as figures by the audience. As Richard Lanham observes:

> The whole of rhetorical training aims at making us aware of the figures and thus ready, willing and able to notice them ... how can figures work their will upon us unless we *do* notice them, at least to some degree? How, for the matter of that, can any *metaphor* work unless we notice it as such? (1991: 158)

On the surface, *Rear Window* seems simple and straightforward in its arrangement (linear time, four consecutive days and an epilogue)[1] and style (unobtrusive, containing minimal optical effects and a gradual, barely noticeable progression towards shorter takes). But it is teeming with complex, almost subliminal, editing patterns which tend towards defying the notion that rhetorical figures are intended to be easily recognised by the audience. However, although the film certainly gives the impression of a classical style, there are a number of infringements of continuity rules for emphatic purposes.

Broadly speaking, although this could equally well be said of many films, there is a dialectic of noticeable cuts and 'hidden' cuts. Because virtually every other cut is to a shot of Jeff watching, and watching not just his neighbours, but also Lisa, Stella and Doyle in his own apartment, we are lured into taking it for granted that Jeff's gaze is omniscient and not simply dominant, but unique.

The spatial organisation of *Rear Window* seems so straightforward that it almost transcends description and analysis. That the action is confined to Jeff's apartment is only partly true. More precisely, the action is restricted to Jeff's *living-room*, or rather, to *half* his living-room. There are no cut-aways to other parts of the city, but nor are there cuts to the kitchen, the bathroom, or the bedroom. Although the shots are not all from the close vicinity of Jeff's wheelchair, the camera never seems to overstep a certain line.

In terms of figures of rhetoric, repetition and alternation are the ones that stand out. These are complicated by Jeff's involvement: either events are filtered through his consciousness or they are not. Repetition in *Rear Window* is strongly associated with the point-of-view structure which is based on alternation and which is used for emphasis. In literature, emphasis means implying more than is actually stated, for instance by using italics or by repeating a word or a stanza in poetry. This can easily be transposed to film where a shot, thanks to its timing in a sequence, can imply more than is actually shown. It does not distort but highlights. What needs to be clarified at this juncture is that by repetition, I do not mean it in its strictest sense; I do not mean that a shot is iterated *exactly*, but rather that the camera set-up is repeated. There are many instances of this type of emphasis, for example in John Woo's films, but it is an unusual device. Moreover, repetition and alternation often merge: similar shots of Jeff looking off-screen (using identical *shot scales\**) are repeated several times but also alternate with shots of the Thorwalds' windows. In some cases, the latter shots are repeated (when identical shot scales are used), but in other cases they are not (when a variety of shot scales is used). But emphasis can be placed in other ways that do not resort to repetition or alternation, for instance the frequent technique of cuts to a closer shot scale, sometimes involving a *jump cut*\*.

There are three types of emphatic shift in shot scale: emphasis on the speaker; emphasis on the listener or the reaction; and emphasis on the action.

## The point-of-view structure

In his statistical study of film techniques over the decades, Barry Salt has noted that: 'Alfred Hitchcock used the point-of-view shot far more than other directors, even those making the same type of film, and in fact such cuts make up about half of his rather high proportion of reverse-angle cuts' (1992: 237). Salt then undermines the importance of his statement by adding that the point-of-view shots 'can obviously be related to the voyeuristic strain in his personality ... not to mention the fact that this device is simply a good way of securing audience involvement, and so it is really in need of no further explanation' (Ibid.). The point-of-view structures in *Rear Window* are certainly appropriate to the narrative, thus making the film one of the major point-of-view films – one that succeeded, unlike *The Lady in the Lake* (1946). However, the assumption that point-of-view shots systematically encourage spectatorial 'identification' with a character is perhaps a little facile.

It is impossible to address film editing without examining the point-of-view (POV) shot or structure. Noël Carroll's 'Toward a Theory of Point-of-View Editing' in *Theorizing the Moving Image* (1996) bears an enticing title, for theories about point of view seldom mention editing, and vice versa. The very conflation of the two terms consequently appears as a welcome breakthrough. Carroll loosely bases his definition of the point-of-view shot on Edward Branigan's (1984) structure. Carroll's argument is that POV editing exists because it is one of the most effective ways of communicating with 'untutored' audiences in so far as it mimics the natural perceptual behaviour of following another person's glance. The second part of the essay deals with the link between POV editing and the communication of emotion; more specifically, the emotion of the characters portrayed in POV shots. The section jettisons the Kuleshov experiment because it underestimates the power of facial expression. However, Carroll neglects other POV structures, which also involve editing but may not be as easily assimilated by our behavioural patterns. What of sustained or flash POV shots? What of delayed POV shots? What of repetition?

On one level, *Rear Window* centres on the activity of looking, on the eye, on the gaze, providing us with a multiplicity of points of view, many of which are easily detectable. Many of the POV shots can be ascribed to Jeff but there are others to consider: Lisa's, Stella's, Doyle's and Thorwald's, as well as some interesting *dual* or even *triple* POV shots (that is to say that the point of view is shared between one or two characters).

However, on another level, the film also articulates, though more subtly, the unseen, i.e. what Jeff in particular (but not solely) *fails* to see. If *Rear Window* were a tragedy, Jeff's tragic flaw would be his metaphorical blindness and not his voyeurism as some have argued. Nevertheless, having said that the basis of *Rear Window* is point of view, it soon emerges that point of view can also function as a decoy.

We are using Edward Branigan's sophisticated definition and breakdown of the POV shot: 'The POV shot is a shot in which the camera assumes the position of a subject in order to show us what the subject sees' (1984: 103). Branigan has identified six elements distributed in two shots (at least):

*Shot A: Point/Glance*

1   Point: establishment of a point in space (i.e. Who sees? Are they human? Animal? Alien? Visible? Where are they situated in the frame?).
2   Glance: establishment of an object, usually off-camera, by glance from the point (i.e. what direction is the 'point', or subject, looking in?).
3   Transition: temporal continuity or simultaneity (Cut or pan; occasionally a dissolve, in the case of a flashback for instance).

*Shot B: Point/Object*

4   From Point: the camera locates at the point, or very close to the point, in space defined by element A1 above (i.e. the camera takes the assumed position of the 'point' who/which is looking).
5   Object: the object of element A2 above is revealed.
6   Character: the space and time of elements A1 through B5 are justified by – referred to – the presence and normal awareness of a subject (This is the coherence inscribed within the structure, e.g. out-of-focus or upside-down point/object shot; movement, etc. In some cases, it is unmistakable: Alicia's (Ingrid Bergman) blurred, hungover vision in *Notorious* (1946); 'Buffalo Bill's' red night vision in *The Silence of the Lambs* (1991)).

The POV shot itself almost always implies editing, and as Branigan and William Simon (1979: 147) have rightly observed, it can only be meaningful if it is inscribed in the broader structure of a *chain* of shots. Repetition plays a crucial part in this POV structure.

It is not my intention to list all the POV shots in *Rear Window*, a task which would be lengthy and not particularly useful. This said, it can be productive to categorise them in order to underpin the multiplicity of points of view. As well as ascribing POV shots to specific characters, I have added a category of 'neutral' POV shots, namely those that can be ascribed to two or three characters – dual or triple POV shots. These occur frequently, in scenes where the reverse-angle cuts show two or three characters looking in the same direction. As Tania Modleski has correctly noted: 'Those critics who emphasize the film's restriction of point of view to the male character neglect the fact that it increasingly stresses a *dual* point of view, with the reverse-shots finding both Jeff and Lisa intently staring out the window at the neighbours across the way' (1988: 80).

*Rear Window* is set over four days (excluding the epilogue). I have listed the instances of POV shots which occur in each:

*Wednesday*: Out of 63 POV shots, 59 are Jeff's and 4 are dual POVs with Lisa, when they both observe – and comment on – Miss Lonelyhearts and Miss Torso.

*Thursday*: 16 POVs, 9 of which are Jeff's and 1 Lisa's, of Thorwald tying rope around a trunk. At this juncture, it cannot be Jeff's POV for he is watching Thorwald through his binoculars, yet the point/object shot is not enlarged or haloed. The remaining 6 POVs are dual – Jeff with Lisa or Stella.

*Friday:* The POV shots become more varied. Out of 50, 23 are Jeff's, 6 are Doyle's and 21 are dual (with Lisa or Stella). Interestingly, Doyle does not look only at the neighbours but also at Lisa's shadow and her case of nightwear. Regarding the two POV shots across the courtyard, we know, despite the angle (the same as in Jeff's POVs), that they are from Doyle's POV because the cuts back to Jeff show him looking, off-screen, *at* Doyle and not *with* him. Just as Jeff looked at Lisa looking at Thorwald on Thursday evening, so Jeff now looks at Doyle looking out, but is now more interested in Doyle than in what Doyle can see. On Thursday, Lisa admonished him with the words, 'Jeff, if you could only see yourself!' and this is what he has begun to do. This shift in viewpoint (from seeing others to seeing himself as 'seer' to being seen) anticipates Thorwald's POV of Jeff on Saturday.

*Saturday:* The POV shots here are significantly shorter takes: this is the day which contains the least dialogue and the most action. Out of 75 POV shots, 31 are Jeff's, 7 are Stella's, 4 are Thorwald's, 1 is Lisa's and 32 are dual or triple. In addition, there are two crucial shots from 'nobody's POV': the camera position and shot scale are identical to those in con-firmed POV shots but reverse-angle cuts reveal that nobody is looking. Of course, these cannot be classed as POV shots at all, but they neverthe-less highlight, through their repetition of camera set-up, the significant *absence* of any point of view. The first occurs after Jeff has looked up Thorwald's number in the telephone book. A three-shot of Stella, Lisa and Jeff records nobody looking in the direction of the window. Cut to a shot of Miss Lonelyhearts' window: she is ominously lowering the blind, causing suspense by making us aware that we know more than the three charac-ters and that Miss Lonelyhearts' life is in danger. The second instance is even more suspenseful: Lisa has been arrested by the police in Thorwald's apartment. Jeff's main preoccupation is to bail Lisa out and with the help of Stella, fumbles around in the dark for some money. Both are turned away from the window. Cut to a shot of Thorwald leaving his apartment. It is a short take: Hitchcock does not want us to dwell on it, but even if we do not understand the full meaning of the shot straight away, Thorwald's slow and ponderous ascent of Jeff's stairs comes as no surprise: we immediately know who the visitor is. It also makes Jeff appear more vulnerable than before. He cannot see everything all the time, he is only human and this makes us empathise with him even more. Similarly, Thorwald's POV shots confer him with humanity and normality: this killer can be blinded by flashbulbs like anyone else. Thorwald's momentarily blinded vision is signalled by his POV shots of Jeff, haloed in red. More importantly, for the first time in the film, Jeff is seen as another person sees him. As Robert Stam and Roberta Pearson have observed, the flashbulb POV shots 'mark Thorwald's "takeover" of the point of view, and in this sense form an integral part of the film's structure of inversions and reversals' (1983: 142). From the moment when Jeff realises that Thorwald is coming to confront him, Jeff loses his point of view altogether. The epilogue contains no POV shots at all, just the pan around the courtyard from 'nobody's POV', or rather, an authorial vision.

Crucially, as the week progresses, Jeff's point of view gradually gives way to other viewpoints. On Saturday evening, when both Stella and Lisa are present, Jeff produces a slide of the flowerbed taken two weeks earlier and compares it to the current state of the flowerbed, concluding that the dog must have unearthed something incriminating. We see Jeff holding the viewer to his eye, then looking off-screen left, and repeating this process four times but we do not see *what* he sees. He then passes the viewer to Lisa whose POV is shown twice as she compares the two views of the flower bed. Jeff takes back the viewer and compares the views three more times, but we are still not shown his POV. Finally, he hands the viewer to Stella, whose POV is shown just once.

This is a subtle but telling way of drawing attention to Jeff's gradual loss of visual control. At the beginning of the film, his point of view prevails; at the end, it is replaced by Thorwald's. When Lisa is in Thorwald's apartment, Stella's POV is unequivocally shown when she borrows Jeff's telephoto lens to check on Miss Lonelyhearts: the shot is quite close and has a black blurred edge. All in all, Jeff is not the only observer (or 'voyeur') in the film. When Jeff is shown hanging out of his window, the shot could quite conceivably be from the viewpoint of one of the courtyard residents.

What does all this reveal? First and foremost that although Jeff's point of view is, by far, the dominant one, which is entirely logical since he is the film's protagonist, it is by no means the only one. However, there is also the possibility, strange though it may seem, of the existence of the *room's* POV. After all, the film's title refers to a specific window and not a character. Moreover, the dual Lisa-Jeff POV shots undermine the notion that Lisa is passive and unseeing. The POV shots chart Jeff's mutation from seeing-subject to seen-object. Jeff soon becomes aware that he too could be watched; in the electrifying telephoto-lens POV shot of Thorwald on Saturday, he realises that he is being watched, and finally, he is seen through Thorwald's subjectivity. Jeff unwillingly ends up following Stella's/ *Reader's Digest*'s advice: 'What people ought to do is get outside their own house and look in for a change.'

*Rear Window as a critique of the Kuleshov effect*

As previously stated, the basis of *Rear Window* is point of view, but, crucially, point/object shots alternate with point/glance shots, reaction shots of what Jeff (and others) see. Illustrative of what Murray Smith calls 'the fallacy of POV' (1995: 156), the cuts back to Jeff contribute as much, if not more so, to our construction of Jeff's character, our 'identification' with him. In other words, POV shots *per se* do not reveal what a character is thinking, although they can draw attention to a shift in attentiveness or interest. Reaction shots, on the other hand, can clarify, and develop, a potentially obscure point/object shot. All in all, the POV shot 'is not nearly as central to "identification" as critics often assume' (Smith 1995: 161). The high proportion of Jeff's reaction shots confers a spectatorial 'alignment' with Jeff, ultimately leading us to empathise with him despite his faults.

If *Rear Window* is, to a large extent, about inference (Jeff never sees anything incriminating; indeed the most telling event – Lars Thorwald leaving with a woman who is 'not his wife' – occurs when Jeff is asleep), so too is point-of-view editing. So too is the famous but unreliable Kuleshov experiment to which Hitchcock referred in the Truffaut interview and which he seemed to endorse. Hitchcock in fact repeated this, using James Stewart in place of the Russian actor Ivan Mosjoukine:

> He took time out to show James Stewart amiably that actors, if not quite cattle, are at least all pawns in the hand of the film-maker, by editing the same shot of him in at two points in the movie, one at which he is supposed to be looking at a girl undressing (in which of course his expression is read as lascivious) and the other at which he is supposed to be watching a mother and baby (at which point he is taken to be projecting tenderness). (Taylor 1978: 204)

It is difficult not to feel sceptical regarding the Kuleshov experiment, not least because it was destroyed and has now become mythical. According to Vsevolod Pudovkin, Kuleshov allegedly intercut a close-up of Mosjoukine's expressionless face with a shot of a bowl of soup, a child playing with a doll and a woman in a coffin (Kuleshov could not remember the exact content of the shots: it could also have been a semi-naked woman) and projected these to an audience who were reportedly astounded by the actor's virtuosity (1954: 140). But more importantly, as V.F. Perkins has observed, not only is the Kuleshov audience unknown, but other factors, including make-up, camera angle and framing, were ignored in the discussions about the experiment (1991: 106). The experiment claimed to demonstrate that reality can be distorted and manipulated, that Mosjoukine was in fact nowhere near a bowl of soup, a child or a deceased woman and that he was not feeling anything in particular. It is somewhat insulting to actors and amounts to stating that acting skills in the cinema are superfluous: it is the editing which can make or break a performance.

However, there is little evidence of a revised Kuleshov effect in *Rear Window*. The close-ups of Jeff following the shots of Miss Torso do not particularly denote the proverbial 'dirty old man', especially when Jeff is talking on the telephone to his editor at the beginning of the film. On the contrary, up to the moment when he notices a distinct change in the Thorwalds' lifestyle, Jeff watches his neighbours in a rather blasé way, rather in the way that one idly watches television while doing other things.

It is what is unusual, novel (e.g. the newlyweds) or concealed (e.g. the bathing beauties on the roof) which intrigues him, not Miss Torso whom he sees every morning. Moreover, no connection was made between diegetic glance and reaction in the Kuleshov experiment, whereas the whole of *Rear Window* rests on this connection.

If anything, then, the Kuleshov experiment is far from being taken for granted and has more detractors than champions. Jean Mitry went so far as to call it 'anti-cinematic' despite being visual because the conflation of images triggers an emotion from an idea (bowl of soup = hunger, dead woman = grief) when they should trigger an idea from an emotion (the Mosjoukine character has not eaten for days, sees a bowl of soup and feels faint). On a cognitive level, Mitry argued that a shot of Mosjoukine followed by a shot of a semi-naked woman would not necessarily conjure up the idea of 'sexual desire' in a child, and that there is nothing factual, let alone contextual about it (1983: 72). Similarly, Noël Carroll argues that the Kuleshov experiment does not correspond to the typical structure of POV editing:

> For the standard POV editing uses the character's face to give us information about her emotional state with respect to what she sees. That is, the character's face is not, as standard versions of the Kuleshov experiment claim, emotionally amorphous, merely awaiting emotive shaping from ensuing shots. (1996: 130)

This is certainly correct in *Rear Window*: the characters' faces trigger a desire in the spectator (and sometimes in other characters) to see what has caused such an expression. On occasion, the point/glance shot is held just long enough to be tantalising and frustrating, causing us to ask, 'What? *What*?' but we are at the mercy of Hitchcock's timing, the decision, editing-wise, of when to show us the point/object shot. In some cases, this point/object shot may not meet our expectations ... there may be a lot of build-up and very little pay-off.

However, we are sometimes given more knowledge than some of the characters. Besides the celebrated pans of the courtyard while Jeff is asleep ('nobody's point-of-view'), there are instances where we have the satisfaction of being able to predict what a character is looking at. On Friday, Doyle visits Jeff for the second time and shares his discoveries regarding Thorwald. Doyle and Jeff are in long shot from the bedroom side of the apartment. Doyle is standing on the left of the kitchen door with a glass in his hand and Jeff is in his wheelchair on the right, turned away from the window. Jeff holds a backscratcher with which he hits his cast. Diegetic off-screen music begins. After a few seconds, having said all he wanted to say, Doyle moves towards Jeff but looks over his head, off-screen right, with the camera tracking in to reframe them in a tighter two-shot. Neither says a word. Jeff, who had been looking at Doyle during the conversation, turns his head and looks off-screen right, following Doyle's gaze. Cut to a very predictable POV shot (possibly from Doyle's POV, but more probably Jeff's) of Miss Torso dancing. Here, the point/object shot of Miss Torso is not delayed because there is no motivation for delay: the audience *expects* Doyle to be fascinated by Miss Torso.

One sequence in particular challenges the Kuleshov effect. It is one of the climactic scenes in the film, when Lisa enters Thorwald's apartment, and is an excellent example of Hitchcock's control over the audience, via editing, but not *just* editing. It occurs on Saturday evening and the lights are on in both Thorwald's and Jeff's apartments. Let us examine the scene from the moment Stella returns to Jeff's apartment, having dug up the flower bed to no avail. At the beginning of the scene, two 'films' are being shown simultaneously: Lisa in Thorwald's apartment and just beneath her, Miss Lonelyhearts, about to swallow a handful of sleeping pills. Both 'films' are, to a certain extent, out of the diegetic viewers' (Stella and Jeff) control: their only weapon is the telephone (see Appendix A on page 120 for the detailed shot breakdown).

The composer and his musicians can be heard tuning up off-screen. Jeff has just been watching Lisa's 'silent movie' (she stands at the Thorwald bedroom window, facing Jeff's block, and shakes the late Mrs Thorwald's handbag upside-down, with a crestfallen expression on her face) with the help of his 'portable keyhole', the telephoto lens, which now rests on his lap. Jeff is in medium shot on the left of the screen, looking off-screen left. He turns his head round to the left as Stella comes in. The camera pulls back a little as she approaches his wheelchair from the left. A pattern of

1

2

3

4

5

6

7

cross-cutting will begin, alternating shots of Jeff and Stella looking off-screen with the action across the courtyard. What is particularly striking here is Jeff's and Stella's enforced stasis and silence. When Thorwald returns and finds Lisa in his apartment, he grabs her and the pair struggle. We are shown Jeff's harrowed expression at this point.

In this sequence, following Mitry's argument, emotion begets an idea rather than the other way around as in the Kuleshov experiment: Jeff watches in fear as Lisa is manhandled but he is immobilised and so feels frustrated and guilty. The continuity creates suspense for we are made very aware of all these events happening simultaneously: Lisa in the apartment; Miss Lonelyhearts on the brink of suicide; Thorwald returning; Jeff and Stella forced to remain powerless.

The Kuleshov experiment was presumably silent. Here, however, sound is paramount: in three shots, Lisa calls out to Jeff, which is ineffectual since there is nothing Jeff can do except call the police, which he has already done with the intention of reporting Miss Lonelyhearts, and be forced to listen. Lisa's cries cue cuts back to Jeff to record his reaction which is far from neutral. In a low-angle medium close-up, Jeff is shown putting his hands around his neck and looking down. That way, he cannot see very much but he can still hear the scuffle, and his gesture is one of both powerlessness and a desire to hide, to cover his ears. He seems on the brink of tears.

*Rear Window* is a good example of the influence of sound on the expressiveness of editing. Hitchcock believed that it could be an updated version of the Kuleshov experiment. Yet, as this sequence demonstrates, thanks to the use of diegetic music and dialogue combined with James Stewart's and Thelma Ritter's acting, the film bears little resemblance to the Kuleshov experiment. The shots of Jeff are not of a man with a neutral facial expression – as Mosjoukine allegedly had. Moreover, it is difficult to imagine that, had Stewart looked impassive, we would automatically have construed that shot a) of girlfriend screaming and being knocked about followed by shot b) of indifferent-looking boyfriend resulted in the complex emotions that are at work here, namely anguish, fear, powerlessness, a dented male ego, regression and helplessness, *inter alia*. Stewart's expressive features combined with Ritter's hand-wringing, the angst-inducing lighting, creepy camera angles and the soundtrack create a mosaic from which we infer such emotions. In addition, the shots of Jeff and Stella trigger the spectator's 'affective mimicry', an expression employed by Murray Smith (1995: 98), and empathy for those who, like us, sit and watch, powerless. We the spectators suffer as we watch a spectator suffer.

The cuts back to Jeff do not further the action. However, they are not superfluous either for their effect is two-fold:

- They show us Jeff's suffering and allow us to empathise with him, our spectatorial *alter ego*. He is being tortured in the cruellest way. It is this moment that signals his redemption – for his sadism towards Lisa, not for his so-called voyeurism – rather than his defenestration by Thorwald.
- They point to Hitchcock as the orchestrator of a dual sadism, towards us, the audience, and towards his 'pawn' Jeff, who has failed miserably as pseudo-director: his lead 'actress' has abruptly changed the script and he has lost control, and so 'his desire to be rid of her is abruptly given a form so direct as to be unacceptable: dream has become nightmare' (Wood 1989: 104–5).

Hitchcock, however, is still at the helm and can inflict suspenseful sadism on the audience – he has achieved his aim of directing his viewers as well as his actors. Regarding *Psycho* six years later, Hitchcock admitted: 'I was directing the viewers. You might say I was playing them like an organ' (quoted in Truffaut 1986: 417). He had already mastered this with *Rear Window*.

*The gaze*

No discussion of *Rear Window*, with its emphasis on looking, can ignore feminist film theory, not least Laura Mulvey's seminal article 'Visual Pleasure and Narrative Cinema', published in 1975, which devotes a section specifically to *Rear Window*.

One of Mulvey's arguments is that classical Hollywood cinema, thanks to its illusion of reality – partly through seamless editing – is constructed around a triad of looks: the camera's; the spectator's (both implicit); and the characters' looks between themselves (explicit). However, like some other critics, Mulvey believes that in *Rear Window*, 'the male hero does see precisely what the audience sees ... Hitchcock's skilful use of identification processes and liberal use of subjective camera from the point of view of the male protagonist draw the spectators deeply into his position, making them share his uneasy gaze' (1975: 15). Yet, as we have seen, the POV shots in *Rear Window* can be ambiguous.

This said, Mulvey is correct in asserting that 'cinematic codes create a gaze, a world and an object, thereby producing an illusion cut to the measure of desire' (1975: 16). This explains why so many interpretations of *Rear Window* seem to be tailored to critics' arguments, rather than the other way round. I would like to argue that this 'illusion' is mainly the product of the quasi-seamless cutting. Hitchcock is not a dishonest film-maker; he does not conceal crucial details from his audience. As he said in an interview on the subject of *Psycho*: 'I'm a great believer in making sure that if people see the film a second time they don't feel cheated. That is a *must*. You must be honest about it and not merely keep things away from an audience' (quoted in Cameron & Perkins 1963: 5). Yet, Hitchcock was simultaneously aware of the power of editing, whether seamless or not: 'The average public ... are not aware of "cutting" as we know it, and yet that is the pure orchestration of the motion-picture form' (quoted in La Valley 1972: 24).

What precisely convinces us that everything is seen through Jeff's consciousness? We 'identify' – a problematic term, but perhaps still the best there is – with Jeff from the beginning for several reasons:

- He is a 'victim' (of an accident; of boredom; of Lisa's so-called 'perfection'; of himself) and despite his shortcomings, he sustains our sympathy until the end.
- We cannot help identifying with Jeff also because we are almost constantly in his space, his home. The other characters are merely visitors. Were Jeff and Lisa cohabiting, this would place a different slant on identification.
- *Rear Window* is the antithesis of *The Lady in the Lake*, a film which is almost unanimously (including by Hitchcock himself

(see Bogdanovich 1963)) condemned as a failure. It is a cinematic *tour-de-force* in as much as the entire film (bar the framework of Philip Marlowe's exposition and epilogue delivered directly to the camera/spectator) is shot from the protagonist's – Marlowe's – subjectivity. We see exactly what he sees, as if the camera were Marlowe's eyes. François Truffaut critiqued the film, explaining that: 'The subjective camera is the negation of subjective cinema. ... Therefore, should the spectator feel the need to identify with a character, he will automatically identify with the face whose gaze in the film he has most often met, with the actor who is most often framed in head-on close-ups' (1962: 40). In *Rear Window*, the face that we see most frequently, at quite close range, is Jeff's. It therefore makes perfect sense, following Truffaut's contention, that we should identify with him.

In addition, even though some POV shots are ambiguous, many of the POV shots in the film are unequivocally Jeff's, namely when he is alone or when reverse-angle cuts confirm that the other person(s) in his apartment are not looking as well.

*Emphasis and alignment*

In *Engaging Characters*, Murray Smith divides the vague notion of 'identification' into three components: recognition (the spectator's construction of character); alignment ('the process by which spectators are placed in relation to characters in terms of access to their actions, and to what they know and feel' (1995: 83)), which is cognitive; and finally, allegiance (the moral evaluation of a character by the spectator), which is emotional rather than cognitive, although based on the first two components. Alignment, argues Smith, depends on subjective access (optical and aural POV) and spatio-temporal attachment.

As mentioned earlier, repetition and emphasis can easily overlap. *Rear Window* does not contain much (audible) dialogue. In terms of dialogue, certain sequences are 'silent' but there is always some sort of aural, diegetic information (the sound of traffic, music or voices from other apartments, and so on) which colours visual POV. However, in dialogue sequences between Jeff and other characters (Lisa, Stella or Doyle), emphasis is placed either on the speaker and his or her statement or on the listener's reaction. This is typical of shot/reverse-shot dialogue sequences, and as Brian Henderson (1976) has observed, there is a tremendous difference between a cut *before* and one *after* a crucial line of dialogue. Where Hitchcock departs from the norm is by choosing to cut to a closer shot of the character (sometimes involving an infringement of the *30° rule\**) – who can be either the speaker or the listener – rather than use a reverse-angle cut. This is not confined only to dialogue sequences but occurs also in action or POV sequences. Let us begin with this category.

*emphasis on action:*
Jeff does not view all his neighbours equally: his vision is directed and motivated by his interest. He finds the Thorwalds' windows riveting and this is amply borne out by the variety of shot scales used to chart his growing or fading interest.

*Rear Window* provides examples of more complex POV structures with the cinematic equivalent of the eye's natural adaptative focus. Jeff resorts to aids, such as binoculars and a telephoto lens, but only from Thursday morning onwards. On Wednesday, he depends only on his naked eye to spy on the Thorwalds with shifts in shot scales. Before Wednesday evening, Jeff had only been mildly interested in the Thorwalds, mainly as a handy illustration of his idea of marital 'bliss'. However, that evening, while Lisa is preparing dinner, his interest grows. After observing and commenting on Miss Torso and her court, Lisa retreats to the kitchen, leaving Jeff alone, still turned towards the window. There follows the usual alternation between Jeff looking off-screen and the Thorwalds' windows. Only this time, the action becomes intriguing, and the shots of their windows become increasingly close. The Thorwalds are not simply arguing. In the final shot of the Thorwalds' windows, Thorwald makes a phone call in the living room and Mrs Thorwald gets out of bed and eavesdrops on the conversation. We can hear her voice, but we cannot make out her words, as she remonstrates with her husband who hangs up and stands, forcing her

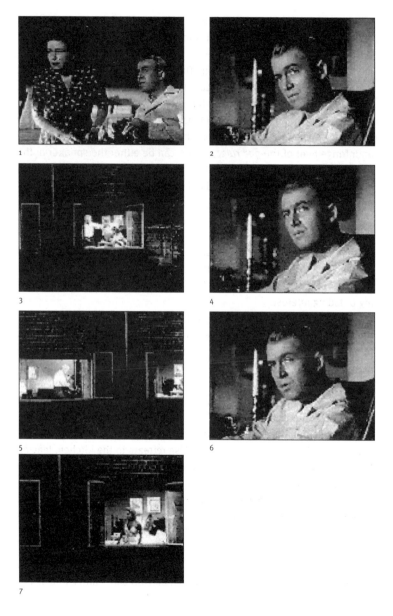

back into the bedroom. The 'Lisa' tune begins off-screen. She finally sits down on the bed, laughing or crying hysterically.

This final shot is much closer and concentrates on just one window at a time, panning when necessary. It is a very simple and effective way of giving us access to Jeff's subjectivity. Four elements are combined: these are not just ordinary POV shots, but POV shots from varying distances. Not that Jeff has moved his wheelchair, but the shift in shot scale symbolically replicates Jeff's desire to witness the scene more closely. In other words, it is the representation of a mental zoom. In addition, there is aural POV: Mrs Thorwald's nagging voice, the police siren (a lugubrious background noise which interferes with Jeff's aural knowledge) and the 'Lisa' tune. The sequence is almost 'silent' in so far as we share Jeff's aural point of view or 'point of listening':[2] he cannot make out the exact words of the Thorwald row from across the courtyard but he can hear the tone of their voices. Consequently, he is obliged to construe information from their gestures.

The soundtrack in *Rear Window* is quite unusual: it is totally devoid of non-diegetic music but it cunningly juxtaposes diegetic music (the radio, the composer rehearsing et cetera), which sometimes plays a non-diegetic role, with specific scenes. For instance, the somewhat melancholic 'Lisa' melody in this sequence fits and enhances the mood of the final POV shot, just as Mrs Thorwald seems to have gained evidence of her husband's betrayal. The 'Lisa' tune will recur, as if by 'accident', at several emotionally-charged moments: for instance, on Wednesday evening, just after Lisa has failed to convince Jeff to lead a more sedentary life or when Lisa is in Thorwald's apartment and Miss Lonelyhearts is about to take her own life but is halted by the music. The important word here is 'juxtaposition'; as Charles Barr has argued, the word 'juxtaposition' is inaccurate to describe montage or editing since these processes involve placing shots *in succession* (1962: 17). However, it is an accurate description of the *layering* of sound and image editing. So what at first appears to be a part-'silent' movie (and this solely because of its realism – Jeff does not have bionic or supernatural hearing) turns out to be a very acoustic film, devoid of 'dead' sound (even at night, there is always ambient noise, much of which is off-screen: foghorns, screeching car tyres, sirens, smashed crockery, a scream, and so on) and where sound plays a key role in provoking many eye-line or 'ear-line' shots. Jeff's interest in the Thorwalds is not exclusively determined by the sound of their rowing, it can also be argued that this sound becomes a reassuring norm and therefore its opposite – silence – will later appear suspicious and ominous, in exactly the same way as Thorwald's decision to stay indoors when the dog is found dead is perceived by Lisa and Jeff as odd. The visual editing rests largely on the cues of the soundtrack and, as we shall see, editing can also be subservient to specific lines of dialogue.

Finally, the tempo is a crucial element in this sequence. The take-lengths of Jeff gradually increase and decrease in proportion to his interest in the action. The take-lengths of the Thorwalds are proportionate to the action to a certain degree (the climax requires 26 seconds to be comprehensible) but they are also anomalous since the closer shots are longer takes despite there being less visual information, and this also confirms Jeff's sustained interest. This contravenes a continuity editing rule which recommends that long shots should be left on the screen longer than medium shots or close-ups (see Bordwell & Thompson 1986).

*emphasis on speech:*
On Wednesday morning, as Stella is massaging Jeff, a closer 'jump' cut draws our attention to something Jeff says. Aside from the noticeable cut, nothing else indicates that his words are important: there is no diegetic or non-diegetic music and Jeff's voice does not change in tone or pitch.

Stella has just told Jeff that she can sense imminent trouble in his life. After some banter about Jeff going to prison for spying on his neigh-

1

2

bours and his 'hormone deficiency', he lies down on his stomach on the day bed, facing the camera in medium-shot. The composer can be faintly heard playing the 'Lisa' tune, which fades when Stella begins to massage Jeff. Stella stands on the left, also facing the camera. Neither is able to make eye contact. While she massages him, he shares his misgivings about Lisa. Once Jeff has settled onto the day bed, the camera remains still. At first, Jeff and Stella are in medium two-shot. They begin to discuss Lisa, whom Jeff sees as 'trouble'. Stella expresses her surprise. 'Jump' cut to Jeff in medium close-up. Stella is still visible except for the top half of her head. Jeff says: 'She expects me to marry her.' Stella answers: 'That's normal.'

The rest of the scene is composed of an alternation between medium close-ups of Stella and Jeff. Because it is somewhat unorthodox in so far as it glaringly breaks the 30° rule, it jolts spectatorial involvement without being heavy-handed (using music, for example). It is worth redefining the jump cut here. Generally speaking, there are two main definitions of this: 'cutting from one time to another or from one place to another with the same camera angle and lens' and 'suddenly changing the angle of the camera or position of the performer in two consecutive shots of the same character', that is, with the camera remaining within an angle of 30° (Konigsberg 1987: 167–8). David Bordwell, in his article on the jump cut, specifies that the most important criteria to define the jump cut as it appears on screen are *continuity of viewpoint* and *discontinuity of duration*' (1984: 5). Admittedly, in the aforementioned scene, there is no discontinuity of duration, which is why I am writing 'jump' cut in inverted commas. This type of 'jump' cut could be renamed the 'forward (or backward in some cases) jump cut' to differentiate it from the other type of jump cut where time has been excised. The forward jump cut here is not disorientating, but it is jarring, especially after a fairly long take. Besides indicating that Jeff does not embrace marriage, it strongly aligns us with him. Let us suppose that the closer shot had been of Stella saying, 'That's normal': we would have been aligned with Stella's appraisal of the 'normality' of marriage, and this would have been an apt illustration of inappropriate or unjustified editing (rather than 'bad' editing, which is an imprecise description).

*emphasis on reaction:*

Remaining on the subject of alignment, we are later granted the possibility of witnessing Lisa's side of the story, as it were. People who enter Jeff's apartment are not shown in close-up until that shot scale can be validated by their proximity to Jeff, in other words, more or less as Jeff can see them, without necessarily being POV shots. Stefan Sharff (1997) has noted that at the end of Wednesday evening, Lisa's confession as she is about to leave ('I'm in love with you') is framed in medium long shot, not in close-up as would be the norm.

However, there are exceptions. Although we do not see Lisa preparing dinner in the kitchen (which would entail a brutal shift in alignment), we are on occasion made privy to Lisa's feelings. This also takes the form of a forward jump cut from a medium shot to a medium close-up. In this example, Lisa is silent. It is her features (as well as Grace Kelly's performance) which are under scrutiny. Lisa is the sort of society girl who tries very hard to hide her feelings. Early on in the film (Wednesday evening), Jeff treats her particularly badly. Thanks to well-timed cuts, we can see how hurt and resilient she is and to what extent Jeff is trying to provoke a break-up.

Lisa enters from the kitchen on the right, bearing a tray. The camera pulls back to medium-shot to include Jeff as she places the tray on the table. Trying to make light conversation, Lisa remarks on the diegetic music coming from the composer's apartment. As she serves Jeff, she says, 'It's almost as if it were being written especially for us.' Jeff, looking off-screen left, answers, 'No wonder he's having so much trouble with it.' This last remark is not that damnable, but whereas Jeff cannot see Lisa's face, we can. There is a jump cut to a medium close-up of Lisa from the same angle. She is visibly taken aback (but only we see her, since Jeff is looking in the opposite direction). She looks down slowly and tries to regain her composure. This jump cut will be repeated when Jeff admits that the dinner is 'perfect ... as always' in a rather negative tone. *Fade** to black on Lisa's tense face as she slowly sits down, her eyes lowered.

Here, Jeff is really pushing Lisa to the edge. The two cuts to Lisa make it abundantly clear that Jeff has touched a nerve, though he is probably not aware of how much he has hurt her. They also reveal where Hitchcock's sympathies lie. Unlike Jeff, the editing treats Lisa like a human being and

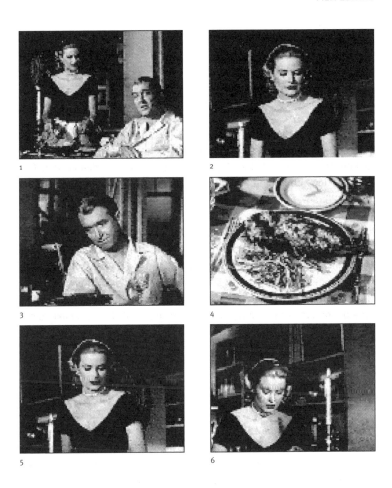

the two cuts are necessary to show that Lisa's stoical silence in the face of such cruelty is nothing more than a front. What is more, the fade-out is on *her* face, making it very clear that she is the character who matters in this scene.

Reverting to Truffaut's argument, what matters in *Rear Window* is not so much who we see, as when we see them. Again, Modleski has observed that Lisa has the final look of the film (1988: 85): she makes sure that

Jeff is well and truly asleep, puts down the travel book she is reading and picks up a copy of *Harper's Bazaar*. Fade to black. In continuity editing, the fade can act as italics: Lisa has made a compromise (she wears unglamorous clothes and is educating herself in the world outside the confines of Manhattan) but she nevertheless has the last look/laugh.

*Rear Window* is perfectly structured, each day ending with a fade to black which emphasises either a look/what is seen or the absence of looking/the unseen. Wednesday morning ends with a fade-out on Jeff as Stella springs up behind him from the kitchen and startles him with the words 'Window-shopper!' Wednesday evening, or rather the early hours of Thursday morning, closes with a fade-out on Jeff asleep, having missed what we have just seen, namely Thorwald leaving with the Other Woman. Thursday ends with a fade-out on Thorwald's dark windows. Friday, the day of incipient reconciliation between Jeff and Lisa (against Doyle), ends with a fade-out on a dual POV shot (Lisa's and Jeff's) of Thorwald's dark window, after the dog's mysterious death. Saturday ends, comically, with a fade-out on Stella's face after Doyle has asked her if she would like to see Mrs Thorwald's head in the hatbox. The Epilogue, as we have seen, closes with a fade-out on Lisa's face.

Most of the fades in *Rear Window* make explicit a character's importance in a scene or sequence, but some function more traditionally as temporal markers. For example, during Wednesday night/Thursday morning, a fade to black separates two identical close-ups of Jeff's wristwatch, registering a time span of half an hour. Fades also indicate a slower pace: there are eight fades on Wednesday, but only two on Saturday when the cutting is more rapid and the action unrelenting. However, many fades spell out what Jeff has *not* seen: his obvious voyeurism, Lisa's feelings, the Other Woman, the reason for Lisa's sudden belief in Thorwald's guilt, and so on. Fades thus confer superiority to the spectator, confirming Hitchcock's claims to respect his audience.

Despite its restricted spatial scope, *Rear Window* is a film about seeing, or failing to see, and this partly explains why it is so cinematic. An examination of its editing strategies allows us to reconsider certain beliefs and fallacies regarding Jeff's omniscience and to question to what extent we are encouraged to align ourselves with him. *Rear Window* may appear admirably simple in its narrative structure, but the editing reveals a more complex aspect which aptly illustrates the oxymoron of film as an 'honest illusion'.

The editing of *Rear Window* relies primarily on two rhetorical figures which occasionally converge: repetition and emphasis. Repetition is created through the use of point-of-view editing, making *Rear Window* one of the great point-of-view movies of all time in so far as it successfully aligns us with the 'voyeur', Jeff. Sometimes coupled with repetition, variations in shot scale monitor Jeff's rising or waning interest in his neighbours. The use of varied shot scales through cutting (sometimes 'jump' cuts) also place emphasis on speech or reactions.

Hitchcock once claimed that one of his greatest fantasies was to observe the reactions of his spectators (see Warren 1989: 25). With Jeff, as well as most of the other characters in the film, as his fictional spectators, he achieved much more than mere observation: he succeeded in analysing these reactions and making them the subject of a film.

### Cuts and uppercuts: Raging Bull

Unlike George Tomasini, Thelma Schoonmaker has gained 'star' status in her field and has given many interviews. Her fame rests primarily on her loyalty to Martin Scorsese. Out of Scorsese's 30-strong filmography (15 feature films, 9 shorts and 6 documentaries), Schoonmaker has edited 15 of his films (10 features, 2 shorts and 3 documentaries) (see Thomson & Christie 1996).

Schoonmaker is well known for her paradoxical editing style that marries the old and the new. Rather like Dede Allen's revolutionary approach in the 1960s and 1970s, Schoonmaker's editing occasionally verges on the 'bad', incorporating jump cuts and the crossing of the axis, but has also received that most conservative accolade, the Academy Award (as well as a BAFTA award) for *Raging Bull*, her first feature.

Schoonmaker's style is recognisable and yet inseparable from Scorsese's influence. Certain critics have argued that she is an 'auteur'

(Faller 1997: 746). Admittedly, one could call *Raging Bull* a 'Scorsese-Schoonmaker' movie, just as one says of *A Matter of Life and Death* (1946) that it is a 'Powell-Pressburger' film or of *Room With a View* (1985) that it is a 'Merchant-Ivory' product. However, Schoonmaker herself adamantly refuses the 'auteur' label and always claims the credit should go to Scorsese since he shoots and edits with her (see Faller 1997). In her interviews, Schoonmaker often speaks in the first person plural rather than the first person singular (see Sherwood 1991). Scorsese and Schoonmaker have even occasionally given joint interviews (Schiff 1996). Given that Scorsese is a competent editor in his own right, it is easy to believe Schoonmaker when she claims that 'when he thinks in the writing and the storyboarding and shooting of the film, he thinks like an editor, so a lot of the conception of the editing is there in his mind originally' (quoted in Sherwood 1991: S9).

*Raging Bull* charts the rise and fall of middleweight boxing champion Jake La Motta (Robert De Niro), also known as 'The Bronx Bull', between 1941 and 1964. The film was entirely shot in black and white bar the title sequence and a home-movie montage sequence.

One key word to describe the editing in *Raging Bull* is 'alternation' which can take the form of a to-and-fro movement between shots or longer segments. Editing structures are generally reliant on alternation and this constitutes one of Raymond Bellour's pivotal axioms with regard to the narrative structures of classical Hollywood cinema (see Bellour 1980). Alternation entails repetition since it implies a *chain* of changes, a succession of changes from one state or action to another and back again *repeatedly*. *Rear Window*, with its point-of-view structures, provided us with an apt illustration of alternation between shots. *Raging Bull*, besides alternation between shots (classical *shot/reverse-shot\** structures et cetera) also contains some evident alternation between scenes, sequences, sound tracks, graphics, speeds and especially, camera movement and stasis. Naturally, the two often overlap, for instance the montage sequences alternate with smoother sequences but also contain alternating shots.

The recurring question, 'where does *mise-en-scène* end and editing begin?' is all the more apposite with regard to *Raging Bull*: often, the two are difficult to distinguish and certainly impossible to divorce and this will be reflected in the analyses: firstly an examination of alternation between shots, paying particular attention to the movement/stasis and slow-motion/normal speed dichotomies (contemplative insert shots will also be examined as disruptive to the alternation patterns, secondly a focus on alternation between sequences and editing styles where the uses of sound editing will be analysed as possible bridges between contrasting styles.

*Alternation between shots*

Thelma Schoonmaker's editing style is characterised by its contrasts. It is by turns seamless and highly visible – she admits to liking both styles (*Premiere* 1996: 42). Her dialogue sequences follow the traditional shot/reverse-shot technique; continuity is often respected; there is an abundance of eye-line matches and matches on action. It soon becomes clear, however, that Schoonmaker plays with these conventions, thereby quelling our initial impression that *Raging Bull* is a 1940s boxing film revisited.

For instance, certain dialogue sequences depart from the norm; some temporal ellipses verge on discontinuity, barely noticeable jump cuts propel the action forward, especially in the fight sequences; establishing shots follow, rather than precede, close-ups, and so on. As Schoonmaker explains:

> At every stage of film-making, Martin hates clichés. Therefore, at the editing stage, we don't do what is 'normally' done. We defuse a dramatic situation, we don't cut to a close-up just because that's what you're supposed to do. (quoted in Assayas & Toubiana 1981: iv)

Scorsese wanted to rewrite the rules by drawing on the past. However, *Raging Bull* does not deliberately set out to break all the rules, rather it provides a good example of an editing style that is at once indebted to and far removed from the film's period look. Scorsese wanted *Raging Bull* to look 'like a tabloid, like the *Daily News*, like Weegee photographs' (Kelly 1991: 125). *Raging Bull* asserts its modernity mainly through the dialectic between period *mise-en-scène* and innovative cutting, or rather cutting that plays with the *mise-en-scène*.

There is a remarkable amount of slow-motion in *Raging Bull*. Scorsese is fond of the technique but nowhere is it used as frequently. In an interview, Scorsese was asked to name his 'master image', a shot which would be emblematic of his entire work. He answered that it would be the opening title shot of *Raging Bull* which records a cowled Jake La Motta, in very long-shot, shadow-boxing in a deserted ring, surrounded by dense smoke (see Ebert & Siskel 1991). The only sound is the Intermezzo from Mascagni's *Cavalleria Rusticana*. Significantly, but also anomalously, the shot is in slow-motion. Anomalously, because Jake is never shown again in slow-motion, except very briefly during the fights. It strips him of his weightiness and brutality and presents us with a misleadingly graceful figure.

At the beginning of the film, Jake is married. He then meets Vickie (Cathy Moriarty), a Bronx beauty who is involved with the Mob. She soon becomes his second wife. Their relationship is a stormy and violent one and Vickie finally divorces Jake. It is generally Vickie who is captured in slow-motion, as seen through Jake's awestruck, desiring and/or analytically paranoid gaze. She is seen once in slow-motion at the swimming pool but more extensively at the Chester Palace dance, which alternates static shots of Jake watching with mobile shots of Vickie. Let us consider this sequence, when Jake notices her for the second time. Jake leaves his wife Irma at home and goes to the dance with his brother Joey. On Joey's instigation, they sit at a table close to the dance floor with three of Joey's friends (see Appendix B on page 122 for the detailed shot breakdown).

A panning high-angle medium long-shot records Jake and Joey greeting friends and sitting down at their table. A priest approaches from the left and shakes hands with the men. An orchestra plays jazz on the left. This is followed by a static medium close-up of Jake laughing. Joey, off-screen, jokingly asks the priest to bless the table. The priest's hands enter screen left and make the sign of the cross. Jake looks off-screen left, then centre left until his gaze is arrested. Cut to an eye-line match POV shot, in slow-motion. Pan left and track forward towards dancing couples moving in the foreground, sporadically revealing a table in the background. Vickie is seated in the middle of a group of people, directly facing the camera. She does not appear to notice that she is being watched but is talking to the person on her right. Dressed in black, with her blonde hair lit from above, she stands out, haloed, from the others. A high-pitched piano melody coincides with the image, as if to underline her fantastic quality. Back to Jake in the same set-up as earlier. He appears transfixed. Cut to a second mobile shot in slow-motion of Vickie, now slightly closer, as if the camera has continued to advance during the previous shot of Jake. This alternation will continue in a chain of six shots, getting ever closer to Vickie. All the shots of Vickie are mobile and in slow-motion. As Vickie and her friends get up to leave, Jake follows her down the stairs and out into the street.

The slow-motion shots are clearly from Jake's point of view, given that the only view that Jake cannot witness, since he is behind Vickie and the group, is in standard motion. However, these are not *strict* POV shots. As Edward Branigan has pointed out, camera *distance* is often inexact in classical POV cutting; camera *angle* is what really matters (see Branigan 1975). But even if these POV shots do not all abide by the POV rule, we nevertheless construe them as POV shots with the help of the soundtrack. Vickie's voice is inaudible, whereas Jake and Joey's whispers can be heard perfectly. Nor can we hear the voices of Joey's friends, yet they cannot plausibly be out of earshot like Vickie. Jake's hearing is extremely selective, and he leaves in the jazz music for it accompanies Vickie like a perfect film score. In other words, Jake witnesses the scene like a silent movie where Vickie is the star and main character and this will be echoed later in the wordless home movies montage where Vickie is dressed like Lana Turner. It is worth mentioning here that slow-motion is frequently used in documentaries on specific film stars.

The editing here expresses both the spatial and symbolic distance between Vickie and Jake's world and their differences of perception: Vickie has evidently not noticed Jake, despite her being a friend of Joey's. It gradually becomes clear that the only possible justification for the movement and slow-motion is that it reflects Jake's point of view, though, as mentioned earlier, not in the strict sense of the term. Just as a camera loves a film star, Jake performs the mental zoom of heightened interest. Even if he does not move physically, his imagination does. Is this his actual vision, or Scorsese's lyrical interpretation? The influence of the cinema on film characters should not be underestimated and this hints at the possibility of a dizzying *mise-en-abîme*: the citation of film techniques not just by the director but also the characters. In other words, it is possible that Jake isolates Vickie in this stylised bubble as a result of having seen films where stars are treated in this way; their bodies celebrated, idolised, decelerated, but also controlled and sometimes muted (as Vickie is in this and the following sequence).

Noteworthy too the *gratuitousness* of the camera movements intercut with the stasis of the shots of Jake. By gratuitousness I mean that the camera movements are not warranted by the movements of the characters. The alternation between typical shot/reverse-shot reminiscent of classical Hollywood cinema, and unjustified camera mobility, points to a reworking of classical conventions. This is an example of New Hollywood editing.

The alternation between Vickie and Jake is frustrating for the spectator. First of all, Vickie is tantalisingly glimpsed *à la* Max Ophuls, behind the obstruction of people walking or dancing in the foreground. Secondly, the cuts back to Jake are perfectly timed to obstruct our view of Vickie even further, for they occur *precisely* when it *could* be possible to see her fully, when the dance floor is on the point of being momentarily vacated. At this juncture, it is Jake who is the obstacle, blocking our field of vision: he sees more of Vickie than we do since the camera has advanced on Vickie during the cuts back to him. From the outset, Jake is established as possessing Vickie. He prevents us from approaching her, just as he will subsequently prevent any man from approaching her. The four reversions to Jake do not just serve as evidence of how mesmerised he is, but also to underpin his spatial dominance.

Finally, these shots of him testify to his normality and immobility. Jake may be quick on his feet in the ring, but out of it, he is often shown sitting or standing, only moving when he really must. In contrast, the shots of Vickie are sinuously mobile and the slow-motion allows her to glide in space and to fully reveal her beauty. They also remove her from the banality of everyday life. As seen through Jake's eyes, she is no ordinary girl from the Bronx, but a supernatural being.

Later in the film, slow-motion shots of Vickie will be used to translate Jake's obsessive jealousy, as in the first Copacabana sequence when

Vickie talks to Salvy and Tommy (this time we hear her words, so we know how innocuous they are), or in the Detroit hotel room when a slow-motion close-up of Tommy kissing Vickie heralds Jake's subsequent fury. Again, these slow-motion shots alternate with standard-motion shots. In this instance, the slow-motion becomes terrifying for it allows us into Jake's deranged mind by dwelling on insignificant details and blowing them out of proportion.

*The treatment of time*

Time and space are manipulated in *Raging Bull* but certainly not enough to be bewildering to the spectator. All 'unnecessary' detail is elided: the 1980s audience is expected to fill in the gaps. Conversely though, some moments are drawn out. There is a scene which captures Jake alone in his dressing-room contemplating his mirror image and soaking his hand in a pail of ice water. It does not further the plot, but it is soothing after Jake's unfair defeat by Sugar Ray Robinson and Joey's fit of anger. Likewise, the series of extreme close-ups of objects which form a motif in Scorsese's films[3] is tantamount to contemplative relief, deflecting from the emotional highs of the narrative. A close-up of a coffee pot and extreme close-ups of a cup and a cup handle at the Debonair Soial Club allow the spectator some respite especially since they follow the violence at the Copacabana. They also constitute a cinephile's (both Scorsese and Schoonmaker come under this heading) moment of 'epiphany'. For Mary Pat Kelly (1980), the epitome of the cinematic epiphany is expressed in the close-up of Jake's blood dripping from the ropes at the end of the final Sugar Ray Robinson fight. If this did not sound religious enough, Pascal Bonitzer goes so far as to use the word 'ecstasy': 'The film often lapses into a sort of gratuitousness, not to say a cinematic ecstasy where the image becomes meaningless and frees itself from the chain of other images, and begins to exist for itself on an abstract level' (1981: 8). These inserts are similar to the parentheses in verbal language, namely words, phrases or sentences inserted as asides, except that their only relation to the rest of the sequence is spatial. In other words, they are not to be interpreted in the same way as the three shots of the stone lions in

49

*Battleship Potemkin*: they are not metaphorical. The shots of the cups, for instance, remain literal. If anything, they constitute a synechdoche – the substitution of a part for the whole – for the setting: coffee-pot and coffee cups = Italian social club; naked light-bulb, empty bottle necks = shabby dressing-room in a second-rate theatre. But it seems to me that these equations are a rationalisation of shots which are, in a sense, superfluous. They have a more important role than supplying us with factual information: they effectively disrupt the rhythm of alternation that we had become accustomed to, in order to sharpen our attention in readiness for the next dramatic high. They also constitute a trope of art cinema conventions; these inserts are digressions which fulfil a citational purpose by referring to another style of film-making. Finally, they alert us to the director's control and choice of what to show us: by embedding these marginal objects within the narrative, Scorsese intends them to bear more significance than they really do (see Perkins 1991: 128). Unlike the stone lions, these inserts are probably later forgotten by the audience, thus privileging more memorable moments, but they will have served their purpose during the film.

Conversely, the fights are speeded up, unlike the fight sequences in another famous boxing movie, *The Set-Up* (1949), which unfold in real time. Similarly, the home-movies montage races through three years and two months in a matter of minutes. Admittedly, only pivotal events (weddings, holidays, new home, children, and so forth) and moments of happiness are recorded or shown. This montage is completely lacking in continuity in the conventional sense: very short takes are spliced together in imitation of the typical home movie's disregard for scale, graphics, movement or motivation.

*Long takes*

As previously mentioned, *Raging Bull* oscillates between smooth long takes and syncopated montage. Scorsese admits to a fondness for both styles: 'I'm torn between admiring things done in one shot, like Max Ophuls and Renoir or Mizoguchi on the one hand, and the cutting of Eisenstein or Hitchcock on the other which I probably love even more' (quoted in Thomson & Christie 1996: 154). While the long takes are by no means extraordinarily long, they nevertheless stand out in contrast to the more rapid editing.

One of the longest takes in *Raging Bull* is mobile and precedes the Marcel Cerdan fight which sees Jake win the championship title. The take lasts 1 minute and 29 seconds. The non-diegetic sound of Mascagni's *Cavalleria Rusticana* is heard throughout, contrasting with the starkness of the setting. It begins in Jake's dressing room with a medium-shot of Joey and Jake in the foreground and the two handlers behind them. The brothers are facing each other and Jake is practising punches on a padded Joey. They stop, Joey briefly exits the frame to discard his padding and helps Jake on with the hood of his robe, then they both move towards the camera, which begins to track back and right to reveal a door frame and a corridor as all four men advance out of the room. The camera continues to track back as they walk down a corridor of the Briggs stadium with Joey walking ahead. Jake adjusts the hood of his robe and shadow boxes. Both look down, not ahead. The camera tracks back round a corner when they turn right, then rises and tilts down a little as they mount some stairs. On the landing they are greeted by a small crowd of spectators who cheer them on. The camera stops as they turn right up more stairs and now tracks forward, tilting up, to follow them into the arena. The changes in background and especially lighting echo the rhythmic changes of montage. The music swells, vying with the audience's cheers and applause. The camera continues to follow them, turning left as they skirt the ring. It finally abandons them and swings up and right to one side of the ring as Jake steps between the ropes on the opposite side. Without stopping, it glides to the right, over the ring in a high-angle long-shot. Cut to a mobile shot (a tilt up) of a radio commentator in medium close-up.

This shot prefigures the celebrated Steadicam shot of the Copacabana club's basement and kitchens in *GoodFellas* (1990). All the hallmarks of that shot are already in place: the music (Mascagni instead of The Crystals) covering the din of the locale (the audience in the stadium instead of the clatter of the kitchens), long corridors with twists and turns, stairs, and the floating sensation imparted by the Steadicam. Both shots

51

signal a peak in these men's lives: Jake is about to win the championship title and Henry has reached the acme in his 'wiseguy' career. The *Raging Bull* take is not as long as the *GoodFellas* one (which totals 2 minutes and 56 seconds), but it is nevertheless noticeable, especially thanks to the mobility afforded by the Steadicam which hints that a positive event is about to happen.

Many medium-long takes, particularly when still, are far less positive. Cunningly, Scorsese does not resort to cutting to close-ups when dealing with domestic violence. These medium-long takes are combined with deep-focus photography to prepare us for the violence. Consider the scene in the hotel just before the Cerdan fight. Jake slaps Vickie for 'showing disrespect' and this is recorded from a distance (in long shot) to include Joey on the right watching the couple, which underlines the triangular aspect of the situation. Similarly, when Jake bursts into Joey's house to beat him up, we are inside the house. Joey and his family are seated around a table in the foreground, eating. We see Jake in the far distance, first through the glass front door, then lunging towards an oblivious Joey. As Lizzie Borden has noted, Jake's domestic violence is all the more terrifying that we witness it 'from the perspective of those on the receiving end' (1995: 61), except that we anticipate it before his victims. A static long or medium-long take fully captures the oncoming violence since the most fearsome aspect of it is its predictability.

The stillness of these shots, as if the camera were rooted to the spot, seems sinister. Scorsese explains that the stasis was used precisely to counteract the excess of the fights: 'With the amount of camera movements and editing pyrotechnics in the fight scenes, I felt that in the dramatic scenes I had to hold back. So the camera moves were simpler' (quoted in Kelly 1991: 136). The domestic violence scenes are far more difficult to stomach than the fights, which become abstract and aesthetic thanks to the rapid cutting and juxtaposition of conflicting graphics and movement. The fight scenes are often filmed as (sports) still photography, striving to capture the balletic movement that characterises most sports. On the other hand, the domestic scenes seem fixed, as if the ring represents the space of freedom, whereas the home is the space of confinement, in reversal of how they really are, or should be.

*Montage*

Much has been written about the eight fight sequences in *Raging Bull*. Models of technical bravura, they took a substantial amount of time to shoot and even longer to mix and edit. Expressionistic rather than realistic, their impact is more aesthetic than harrowing and is far removed from both the experience of watching a real boxing match or the traditional boxing film genre.

All the fights were planned and choreographed to minimise real blows. For each fight, Scorsese drew storyboards which were usually adhered to. Only one camera was used (see Kelly 1991). There are few cuts to the audience and as Scorsese explains: 'I wanted to do the ring scenes as if the viewers were the fighter and their impressions were the fighter's – of what he would think and feel, what he would hear' (quoted in Kelly 1991: 132). The subjective sound and point-of-view shots are not just from Jake's perspective; the final Robinson fight, for example, reveals Robinson's visual and aural subjectivity as much as Jake's.

Schoonmaker was given a free rein to cut the fight sequences as she wished. She explains that for the thirteenth round of the final Robinson fight, she first edited for narrative structure and then reworked the scene for movement, lighting and effects (see Faller 1997). This scene lasts only 1 minute and 52 seconds but contains over fifty shots. I consequently want to dwell on only a few segments. The round can be divided into three parts: the first, which takes us up to Jake beginning to provoke Robinson, remains conventional in its editing, reflecting the ordinariness of the fight at this point. The editing respects continuity: it is shot and cut exactly like a classical dialogue sequence with a shot/reverse-shot pattern over four shots. The second part begins with the long shot of the two men sizing each other up, Jake exhorting Robinson to hit him and Robinson standing still, and continues until the zoom-out/track-in of Robinson is completed. This part shows a departure in style and rhythm. The third part begins with Robinson hitting Jake and ends when the referee steps in to prevent Robinson from killing Jake.

One can hear the sound of the television commentator over the cries of the audience (Joey is watching the bout on television): diegetic and non-diegetic sound merge. The referee walks from behind Robinson and exits screen left. Jake continues to provoke Robinson, who does not move, just sways a little. After this shot, the camera will consistently cross the axis of action, switching from one frontal shot to another. The next five shots are all POV shots, getting gradually closer as Robinson advances towards Jake. This second part signals a significant change in the tempo. The takes in the first part are of medium length: the first two-shot is seven seconds long, but the average length of the remaining shots is three seconds. In the second part, the takes are longer; the final part is characterised by very short takes, many of which are well under a second long. Let us look at the second segment more closely, after the long two-shot.

Frontal medium-shots, very probably point-of-view shots of Jake and Robinson, alternate. The ropes and audience are slightly out of focus in the background. The camera begins to simultaneously and smoothly zoom out and track in. This technique reaches a crescendo in a POV shot of Robinson, as if to reproduce Jake's dizziness and making Robinson, now back- and side-lit by the floodlights, appear threatening. Robinson stares straight into the camera. The section ends with Robinson bouncing forward, looking abnormally larger thanks to the compressed zoom technique. Even more attention-grabbing than the compressed zoom device is the soundtrack. At first, we hear the diegetic sound of the audience and the punches overlaid with the diegetic but external patter of the television commentator. Then, when the zoom/track movement is completed, non-diegetic silence ('dead' sound) takes over. This is not sudden but happens very gradually in the course of the shot. We have confirmation that it is non-diegetic, or at least non-objective, for we can see the audience in the background waving their arms about. Finally, a very faint rumble begins across the next two shots, gradually becoming louder until it explodes into a roar, followed by the diegetic thud of Robinson's punch and the crackle of the off-screen camera flashbulbs.

Thereafter chaos, both aural and visual, breaks out. Sound is distorted, constant flashbulbs light up the screen (which sometimes goes white very briefly) making the editing seem even more rapid than it already is (an excellent example of *mise-en-scène* merging with editing), the 180° line is crossed several times, slow-motion reveals punches that would otherwise

be a blur, the camera cuts back three times to Vickie covering her face with her hands, there is an abundance of high- and low-angle shots and one shot is even almost overhead.

The effect is two-fold: both men's points of view are shown equally, yet the chaotic rhythm, conflicting graphics and subjective sound squarely align us with Jake. It is *his* experience, his distorted perception that we relate to on the screen. The montage constructs what Jake is feeling. The final part amounts to a mosaic with some shots being more memorable than others (e.g. spurting blood; Vickie) while others remain 'invisible', or visible only subliminally. Secondly, this segment is almost unbearably claustrophobic with many close-ups and extreme close-ups, and we may feel that *we* are being attacked by the director. We are consequently simultaneously positioned as participant (Jake, being hit and watched) and as audience (Vickie and Joey, watching and suffering). The montage is by no means realistic but it conveys a realism of perception: Jake's dazed consciousness and Vickie's/Joey's pained (and fragmented, in Vickie's case) vision.

There are several breaks in continuity. For instance, in one shot, Robinson raises his left arm and, in the following shot, Jake receives a blow from the left knocking his head to the right. Similarly, when Robinson causes Jake to spurt blood from the left of his face, in the following shot, the photographers are spattered from the left. These 'errors' are not noticeable at first (or indeed tenth) viewing and add to the sense of turmoil. As Schoonmaker says of the jump cuts in *GoodFellas* (but this could just as easily apply to *Raging Bull*), 'that way you can create effect, and because it's so powerful, people forgive the jump cut' (in Sherwood 1991: S9).[4]

*Sound*

The use of sound in *Raging Bull* is somewhat atypical, particularly in the combination of image and sound editing. Schoonmaker is renowned for her predilection for sound overlaps from one sequence to another and these are particularly appropriate to temper certain hard cuts. The overlaps can be treated as aural dissolves which blend two conflicting shots. This said, there are numerous instances of simultaneous image and sound cuts. These often serve to reinforce the pattern of alternation between sequences, with sound fluctuating from one extreme (barely audible dialogue, no music, sometimes even 'dead' sound) to the other (almost uncomfortably loud noise of punches, crackling flashbulbs and a commentator's voice in the fights). A good example of this aural clash is the scene where Jake wakes Vickie, asleep in their bed, to interrogate her about her throwaway comment regarding Janiro's beauty – very quiet, no music – which is sandwiched between the Copacabana sequence – noisy: voices of Jake, Salvy and Tommy, as well as background hubbub of conversation, clinking glasses et cetera – and Jake's fight with Janiro – very loud, with the cut occurring precisely on the sound of a punch.

Paradoxically, the quieter sequences, particularly when introduced by a straight, simultaneous image and sound cut, are more frightening than the cuts to a loud soundtrack which may cause us to start. Minimal sound, rather like minimal camera movements and editing, becomes synonymous with impending violence and creates a feeling of unease. These hushed sequences, which should be havens of peace in-between the tumult of the fights, are in fact very tense. De Niro's minimalist performance is in keeping with the silence: Jake seldom shouts, and the more he lowers his voice, the more threatening he becomes.

The overlaps, however, are more reassuring and can even mitigate violence by cushioning the cut between contrasting sequences. Consider the end of the second Copacabana sequence where Joey viciously beats up Salvy with the help of a cab door. A static camera records the mayhem in the street in long shot, briefly cutting to a closer shot of Joey clambering over the cab to get away before reverting to the previous long shot, which lasts four seconds. Mascagni's music gradually swells over the shot of Joey, blotting out the sound of the rumpus for eight seconds and continues over the cut (which coincides with a high note) to a static daytime shot of the window of the Debonair Social Club. Night has turned into (rainy) day, a small crowd has given way to a solitary man crossing the screen from left to right, presumably running for cover. Short takes of objects follow (a closer shot of the words 'Debonair Social Club. Members Only' on the window, a framed certificate on a wall, and the afore-mentioned coffee pot and cups). Tommy's gruff voice gradually becomes audible over the music, the latter lasting 45 seconds into this second sequence. The non-diegetic music links the two sequences with a cause/effect relationship, more effectively than a dissolve would have done. *Diegetic* sound overlaps are more usual in the film, however, and signal a temporal leap (backwards or forwards) as well as a cause/effect link, as in the overlap between the opening sequence and the cut to 1941. What is important in the Mascagni example is precisely the choice of *largo* non-diegetic music which soothingly announces the end of this almost comically excessive sequence and gently lowers us into the next. In short, the combination of sound and image editing can be remarkably salient and expressive, either because of the isometric quality of the sound and image cuts or, conversely, because of their disjunction.

In 1980, Martin Scorsese claimed not to be very aware of, or interested in, his audience. *Raging Bull* was voted best film of the 1980s in an American critics' poll and this allegedly came as a surprise to him (see Thomson & Christie 1996). Yet, it seems fair to state that *Raging Bull* is very self-conscious and audience-conscious in its editing and indeed one can even argue that the editing is overtly controlling. *Raging Bull* is a very structured film which makes us aware of the 'Russian doll' aspect of film editing, especially where alternation is concerned; it is like a changing mosaic of small and seemingly disparate pieces which create a cohesive whole. The film chiefly alternates between one state and another, and it is this shift, namely the cut, which raises our awareness of the *mise-en-scène*. The camera's stillness and movement, for instance, can only be truly visible when played against each other.

The editing in *Raging Bull* rests primarily on constant and noticeable change, change *intended* to be noticed, and this noticeability becomes a spectatorial pleasure in itself, besides the pleasures of the black and white photography, the acting and many other aspects of the *mise-en-scène*. *Raging Bull*, like many of Scorsese's films, and also those of other New Hollywood directors (Francis Ford Coppola, Brian de Palma, George Lucas, Steven Spielberg and so on), is pitched to an audience of cinephiles, a knowing audience who are so familiar with the media of film/video/television that they will pick up every little cut, every editing nuance, especially since this type of editing is hardly invisible. It is not *obvious* in the utilitarian sense of certain (Hollywood or other) blockbusters which leave barely any room for ambiguity or contemplation, but it is meant to be seen, bringing Scorsese and his audience into an understanding.

Both *Rear Window* and *Raging Bull* demonstrate a sophisticated understanding of the expressiveness of editing. Both exemplify the effects of cutting between shots of varying depths of focus, which subtly contributes to an overall rhetoric of repetition and alternation. Both Hitchcock and Scorsese are acutely aware of their audience in these films.

Neither of these films is really 'typical' of the classical narrative system: Hitchcock exerted control over his films before auteurism was even recognised and Scorsese's movies are hardly standard Hollywood fare. In her survey of New Hollywood narrative technique, Kristin Thompson (1999) believes that the New Hollywood is not all that different from the Old Hollywood: stories are still clear, coherent and, consequently, appealing. But what of editing? Has it become more sophisticated, less 'simplistic' than the continuity editing of the past? Or are we posing the wrong question to begin with? It transpires from many classical Hollywood films that many of them were not so conventional in their editing after all: they often broke the rules, they often 'cheated', for emphatic and expressive purposes. They were less rigid than we like to think. Consequently, New Hollywood editing has not been revolutionary. Certainly, *Raging Bull* demonstrates that, thanks to the influence of European art cinema conventions and audiences' growing awareness of the auteur, editing in the New Hollywood has become more visible. Nevertheless, the common denominator in both Old and New Hollywood is that editing has a clear and definite purpose in mind which is made transparent to the spectator: these films welcome analysis, they are 'readerly', to borrow Roland Barthes' term (1970: 10). However, as we shall see in the next chapter with *A bout de souffle*, European art cinema is far more ambiguous and 'writerly' about stating its editing motivations and goals.

## 2    ART CINEMA AND THE AVANT-GARDE

Art cinema is generally perceived as being 'European', although this is misleading. It is taken to be an alternative to the classical narrative system. For instance, resolution is not always apparent and the narrative is more loosely structured, containing digressions. Furthermore, departures from linearity, such as flashbacks, are not always clearly signposted, and character motivation or goals are often lacking or unclear. It is generally a cinema of auteurs, bearing their personal hallmark and vision. Finally, continuity editing rules can be violated, generally deliberately in order to jolt the viewer.

As we have seen in the previous chapter, certain sequences in *Rear Window* revealed that jump cuts do not necessarily disorientate the spectator and can be absorbed into the film's spatial continuum. However, there are different ways of breaking the rules of continuity editing. Schematically, these can be divided into three categories: unintentional 'hiccups' (or at least, one assumes that they are unintentional); intentional (to do away with 'dead time' or the examples cited from *Rear Window*); and a curious mixture of both, which characterises Jean-Luc Godard's *A bout de souffle*. It is not my purpose to dwell on the accidental dimension of the genesis of *A bout de souffle*'s editing, although this will be touched upon, but rather to focus on the end product and how this seemingly clumsy and amateurish film has earned such a reputation as a watershed in editing style.

Energetic, jagged, shoddy... These adjectives recur frequently in discussions about the editing in *A bout de souffle*. In the wake of its release, the film was vilified by the *Positif* critics, Godard's detractors, mainly for its editing style, which made the film appear 'butchered' and which set the tone for a 'rough-draft cinema' (Graham 1968: 163). To these critics, the film was riddled with the cinematic equivalent of linguistic solecisms, i.e. the ignorant misuse of cases, genders and tenses; it was the visual counterpart to an incompetently translated instruction manual.

This case study is divided into three sections: the first will address the discontinuity of the film and will touch upon Godard's filmic rhetoric; the second will look at the oft-mentioned jump cuts, their genesis and effects, and the final part will examine the use of long takes.

*Discontinuity and the reinvention of conventions: 'Allez vous faire foutre!'*

Before the New Wave, French cinema used a type of continuity editing similar to the Hollywood model, with the difference that French continuity editing displayed a greater fondness for longer takes and a more limited reliance on shot/reverse-shot and close-ups (see Vincendeau 1992).

*A bout de souffle* flaunts its spatial and temporal discontinuity from the very first frames. Virtually every other cut in the film is unmatched. In 2002, after repeated viewings, it is difficult to imagine how the 1960 audience responded to this overt avoidance of conventions, but it is probably safe to affirm that many spectators would have found the opening sequence, for instance, audacious and somewhat bewildering, though not so much in terms of narrative (even film-illiterates can understand what is going on), but in terms of its reasoning and function.

The film begins without a credit sequence, just the title, in tall white letters on a black background, which fills the screen. The title is preceded by a dedication to Monogram Pictures, famous for B-movies, if not Z-movies, an insult to good taste in itself. The very first shot is not an establishing shot but a static medium close-up of a newspaper, or more precisely, the drawing of a scantily-clad pin-up holding a doll. A sleeve is visible on the right of the screen. We hear the off-screen words, 'Après tout, j'suis con. Après tout, si, il faut, il *faut*!' ('All in all, I'm a stupid

1

2

3

4

5

6

7

8

bastard. All in all, yes, you've got to'). The paper is lowered to reveal the title 'Paris-Flirt' and Michel Poiccard's (Jean-Paul Belmondo) face, the brim of his trilby at first obscuring his eyes. He is smoking a cigarette. He looks up from under his hat, then glances off-screen centre-left, then right. He rubs his lips pensively with his thumb. Cut to a static close-up of a dark-haired woman who looks off-screen left, then right. Looking off-screen right, she nods, presumably at Michel, but we cannot be sure at this juncture. A foghorn sounds. This pair of set-ups will be repeated, more briefly, containing the same nods (though more emphatic) and the background sound of the foghorn. This is followed by a medium long-shot of a parked Oldsmobile. A couple get out of the car with the camera panning right to follow them walking away. It will gradually become clear that the two characters do indeed know each other and are conniving to steal the Oldsmobile, and that the sequence is set in Marseilles. It is only in the last shot of the sequence that the two characters and the car are in the same frame.

This is a prime example of Godard's rejection of traditional spatial continuity. Temporally, the sequence is continuous; the events are consecutive, not shuffled. However, there are ellipses (we do not see Michel walking towards the car) although these are not substantial enough to be disconcerting. Most of the shots are static, mimicking the stillness of the wait, the perfect timing of the theft. This said, the first eight shots, that is to say, before we gain confirmation that Michel, the woman and the car are within the same space, are unusual in so far as we are given a composite picture which is less clear that to which we are accustomed to. As it is, the first eight shots are suspenseful given Godard's control of the events. Though occurring in chronological order, the characters and events are spatially disconnected and the eye-line matches lead nowhere: the woman looks at something/one then at something/one; so does Michel; but what, and/or whom are they looking at? The scene relies extensively on *false* eye-line matches. The lack of guidance prompts the spectator to ask questions such as: Where are we? Is this man talking to himself? Why? Do these people know each other? and so on. It is difficult, if not impossible, to imagine off-screen space coherently. Godard is subverting our attempts to reorganise the matches. Aurally, from the sound of the foghorn, we know that the scene is unfolding by the sea. Michel's background is a spatial dead-end since it is a gridded shop window. Crucially, the ninth shot could be termed an establishing shot. It records a fishing boat in long-shot with Marseilles' landmark, Notre Dame de la Garde, briefly and faintly visible in the background, but it nevertheless refuses to place the two characters and the car in the same frame. An establishing shot at the onset of the film would have been the norm in French cinema at the time. Here, the film opens with a medium close-up of a *newspaper*, not even a character, and a disembodied voice which tells us nothing: Is it internal monologue? Voice-over? His off-screen voice? Does it belong to the person holding the paper? (Jean-Paul Belmondo was only a budding actor at the time and his voice would not have been widely recognisable). Reisz and Millar argue that 'in a way Godard is confessing that he knows as little about this man as we do' (1996: 351). I would argue, on the contrary, that Godard knows his hero inside out, his alter ego as it were, but that does not mean that he should disclose everything: the spectator must participate to bring the film to life. And it works: our attention is held and we want to find out more.

Although concise, the sequence contains details which are extraneous to the plot: the old fishing boat is not an agent in the action, but confirms our suspicions that the locale is on the coast. However, only spectators familiar with Marseilles are able to recognise the Vieux Port. There is no title (such as 'Marseilles: August 1959') and there are no clues in the dialogue. Does it matter? It matters in the following sequence, as we shall see. In short, this opening sequence jettisons the conventions of continuity editing but it is not baffling. It leaves certain questions open without frustrating us. It is a perfect example of Godard's decision to make a film 'without rules and whose only rule would be that the rules are wrong or badly enforced' (Godard 1980: 29), but not illogical or incoherent for all that.

The second sequence, which unfolds on the road between Marseilles and Paris, the Route Nationale 7, disrupts both spatial and temporal continuity. Again, this is neither bewildering nor disorientating despite certain gaps. The latter half of the sequence, from the moment Michel catches sight of the two motorcycle policemen, breaks most of the rules of continuity editing:

- the 180° line is crossed
- the 30° rule is transgressed
- graphics are conflicting
- there are 'leaps' between shot scales

Classical action sequences often stray from the conventions for purposes of dramatic intensity, but this scene is extreme. However, as Reisz and Millar have argued, the chase leading up to the murder of the policeman is easy to follow: '[It] is not baffling; except for a couple of curious changes of direction, we can follow the action perfectly clearly ... What the extract here shows is that Godard does not flout logic but rather pushes it further towards its extreme' (1996: 350).

The scene is very rapid and some camera movements are so quick as to be almost invisible (see Appendix C on page 123 for the detailed shot breakdown). Unlike many action sequences, this one is not spun out. Some events are missing: time must have elapsed between the penultimate and final shot. Also in shot 4, the jump cut excises a few seconds of the action. Interestingly, few spectators find the change of direction in shot 6 problematic. We do not assume that the policemen have given up the chase and have decided to go home. Within the context (we did not see them slow down), we assume that they were recorded from the other side of the road. We respond to the scene as if it were authentic, a documentary. However, the documentary style is soon contradicted by the dramatic music and the extreme close-up of Michel and the gun. Similarly, discontinuity is not a constant: there are eye-line matches (shots 10 and 12) and aural pointers (the sound of the motorbikes, Michel's mumblings which alert us to the presence of a police patrol and the stalling of the car).

So although Godard does not provide us with many clues or the possibility of omniscience, a lack which could be construed as disrespectful to the audience, he does not underestimate the audience's intelligence. What at first seems tantamount to a 'bras d'honneur' ('V' sign) to the audience, spoon-fed on 'easy' cinema, could be read, on the contrary, as a sign of connivance, and this ambivalence sets the tone for Godard's subsequent relationship with his audience. In *A bout de souffle*, he avoided the pitfall of opacity while inviting the spectator's active involvement.

In *Introduction à une véritable histoire du cinéma*, Godard articulates the problem of audience knowledge. If rhetoric involves pitching a film to a specific audience, then Godard seems to be mystified by the concept of filmic rhetoric. He claims that he finds it impossible to imagine or visualise an audience and was consequently taken aback by the resounding failure of *Les Carabiniers* (1963). He writes that he makes films to fulfil a personal need that extends beyond the requirements of box-office success: 'We talk endlessly of the spectators, but I don't know these spectators, I never see them, I don't know who they are' (1980: 70). Reisz and Millar argue that 'At first sight, he appears never to have heard of the dangers of boring or offending his audience' (1996: 346). This is admittedly true, but I think few people would agree that *A bout de souffle* is boring or so offensive that it is impossible to stomach. Some have mentioned the pleasure of the film, pleasure of its rapidity, of its energetic jump cuts, of the unpredictability of the editing, of its movement; others have mentioned the poetry in the reinvention of filmic language, a sort of anastrophe, a rhetorical figure, i.e. an unusual arrangement of shots for poetic effect. This pleasurable editing has remained resolutely modern.

The contemporary reviews claimed that the redeeming feature of this 'botched' editing was its energy. *Variety*, for example, noted that it 'uses a peremptory cutting style that looks like a series of jump cuts ... But all this seems acceptable for this unorthodox film moves quickly and ruthlessly' (27 January 1960: 6). Also very energetic is what Dudley Andrew calls the 'quick cut' (1987: 11), i.e. a shot of a static figure followed by one in full motion. These are legion and Godard, in a recent interview, explained how they were created:

We decided to do it mathematically. We cut three seconds here, three here, three here, and later I found out I wasn't the first director to do that. The same process was described in the memoir of Robert Parrish, who was an editor on Robert Rossen's *All the King's Men* (1949) ... Parrish told Rossen, 'Let's do something different. We'll look at each shot and we'll keep only what we think has more energy. If it's at the end of the shot, we'll throw out the beginning. If it's at the beginning, we'll throw out the end.' They did exactly what I did later, without knowing what they had done. Only, I said, 'Let's keep only what I like.' (quoted in Dixon 1997: 16)

The quick cuts achieve speed without confusion, even though there is often a jarring change of direction (for example when Patricia (Jean Seberg) buys the paper before turning in Michel), and confer a feeling of panic (for instance, in the final sequence, there are three quick cuts before Michel is shot).

Another alternative to continuity editing is articulated in Godard's seemingly arbitrary arrangement of shot scales. There was already evidence of this break with convention in the cop-murder sequence where an extreme close-up of the barrel of the gun is sandwiched between two medium long-shots. One of the most striking and exciting aspects of *A bout de souffle* is the coexisting, and sometimes conflicting, interpretations that it can yield. It is perfectly feasible to simultaneously feel that one has understood the reasoning behind a cut and to doubt that reasoning, to feel disturbed by the possibility of a hoax, that one has in fact been taken in by Godard's flukes and short cuts. Nevertheless, even when one is aware of the offhand way in which much of the film was made, it is still impossible not to interpret it. Consider a choice of shot scale which illustrates this ambivalence: it is quite subtle but eloquently signals a shift in character alignment and, interestingly, bears a remarkable similarity to certain scenes in *Rear Window*.

Like Hitchcock's film, *A bout de souffle* opens on the male character and closes (also with a fade to black) on the female character, although Patricia, unlike Lisa, stares straight into the camera before turning round. Both films centre on the male character but also allow brief incursions into the subjectivity of the female character. In *Rear Window*, changes in shot scale (using jump cuts) lead us to align ourselves with Lisa when Jeff is being catty towards her. Similarly, near the end of *A bout de souffle*, a close-up of Patricia listening to Michel and Antonio Berruti (Henri-Jacques Huet) talking off-screen indicates that she is more than just listening to the dialogue.

Michel and Patricia are looking for Berruti in Montparnasse. They finally locate him about to take blackmail photographs in a café. The first shot is a static medium shot of another acolyte, Carl (Roger Hanin), with Patricia and Michel. Carl criticises Michel for wearing silk socks with a tweed jacket. Berruti enters screen left and Carl leaves screen left. Berruti's girlfriend walks over from the left and stands next to Patricia. Jump cut to a close-up of Patricia from the same angle. She looks off-screen left at Berruti, who, off-screen, addresses Michel. Although it is clear that Berruti is speaking to Michel, at first it seems that he is addressing Patricia, because the cut to her face and Berruti's words coincide. Michel answers Berruti. Cued by Michel's response, Patricia looks off-screen right at him. Patricia follows the conversation with her head, looking left and right again. Cut to a tight medium shot of the four characters, as in the first shot.

The close-up jolts us to take notice. The dialogue between Carl and Michel or Berruti and Michel is banal and does not further the action but the close-up announces a change in Patricia as well as emphasising her role as a mere listener. She is the ignorant outsider who cannot really help. But, more importantly, it draws attention to her presence and her possible feelings. Perhaps this interpretation takes liberties with what is, after all, 'just' a close-up. Nothing in Michel and Berruti's exchange can possibly lead us to believe that she is plotting to turn him in to the police. Her face expresses very little, it is even quite amused and kindly. If this were a four-shot, we would not be tempted to place so much meaning on her, but the close-up crystallises her subjectivity. We cannot know what she is thinking, what matters is that the *possibility* of her thinking something has been highlighted. This shift reveals the ambivalence of her feelings for Michel well before her more explicit hesitation (by staring intently at him) in the Swedish model's apartment. She has become part of his circle of underworld accomplices, and although she may temporarily be drawn to that milieu, she is a staid, law-abiding bourgeoise at heart. It is the first time that we are invited to become involved in Patricia's plight, except for a brief moment in her bathroom, when, alone, she contemplates and talks to her reflection in the cabinet mirror. From this moment on, the film privileges her story over Michel's who becomes the object of her momentous decision.

Finally, Godard's defiance of continuity editing is perhaps best epitomised by his use of the black screen, an iris-out held for longer than normal. Roy Thompson, in *Grammar of the Edit*, stipulates that a mix of any sort (*dissolve\**, *iris\**, fade, and so forth) should last for a minimum of one second and a maximum of three seconds (1996: 52). The iris-out in this sequence lasts seven seconds. This occurs 18 minutes into the film, immediately after Michel has spoken to Tolmatchoff in the travel agency. Having succeeded in evading the two detectives, Michel stops outside a cinema and gazes at a still of Humphrey Bogart in *The Harder They Fall* (Mark Robson, 1956). A reverse-shot shows Michel looking at the still off-screen whilst rubbing his lip. A cut records Michel in medium shot striding off to the right. The camera pans to follow and then leaves Michel to exit screen right while it stops to capture the distant reflection of the detectives, looking confused, in the cinema's glass door (six seconds). Iris-out on the two men. This is followed by a black screen which lasts seven seconds. Michel and Patricia's voices, as well as non-diegetic music, can be heard on the soundtrack:

MICHEL (off): J'ai vu un [*music begins: slow xylophone*] type mourir. [I saw a guy die.]

PATRICIA (off): Pourquoi mourir? [How did he die?]

MICHEL (off): Dans un accident. [In an accident.]

PATRICIA (off): Tu m'invites à dîner, Michel? [Are you taking me out to dinner, Michel?] [*Iris-in to an extreme close-up of Michel's outstretched palm holding a few coins*]

MICHEL (off): Evidently!

The camera pans left and tilts up to reveal the rest of Michel, pocketing the money. Cut.

The noticeable length of the black screen serves to remind us that sound and image can be divorced (as is taken further in *A bout de souffle*'s counterpart, *Pierrot le fou* (1966)). The black screen is at once the negation and the beginning of the cinema. The use of the iris-out/in serves to exhume archaic optical effects, but the black screen takes this return to the source a step further. It is equivalent to a Cartesian *tabula rasa*, the opposite of citation (e.g. iris = Griffith or Welles) or a nod to the past, rather it is the black slate that has been wiped clean, the state of solip-sism. However, the slate has only been wiped visually, for the soundtrack continues to be 'alive'. We are consequently very aware that we are watching a film, that this is intentional. The black screen in conjunction with sound draws attention to the (shrouded?) camera, in the same way that the jump cuts and the characters or passers-by staring at the camera relentlessly drag us back into reality, a cardinal sin in the Tradition of Quality era which preceded the New Wave, also known more pejoratively as the *cinéma de papa*.

*Jump cuts: 'Vivre dangereusement jusqu'au bout!'*

It has now become a cliché to state that Godard's cinema is 'Brechtian', namely that it shares with Berthold Brecht's theatre a certain self-cons-ciousness, which has a distancing – *Verfremdung* – effect on the spec-tator. This is never so apparent as in the sequences or scenes containing a quick succession of jump cuts.

It is easy to forget that jump cuts have always been with us, from George Méliès and Vsevolod Pudovkin to the present, mainly because most of them are not all that disruptive. There are two types of jump cuts: very brief temporal ellipses, where the camera does not move at all (which accounts for most of the jump cuts in *A bout de souffle*), or leaps in space, where the camera moves, but by no more than 30°. What is particularly different, and ultimately shocking, about many jump cuts in *A bout de souffle* is that they are so patently gratuitous. Elliptical cutting is commonly used to excise 'dead time', thus speeding up the action, and indeed there are instances of this type of ellipsis in *A bout de souffle*, for example the scene with Patricia in the car which is analysed below. But other jump cuts, especially the one-off variety (i.e. an entire scene or even sequence containing just one or two jump cuts), are mystifying and often seem unnecessary, given that they shorten the film by only a few frames at the very most. In other words, there was nothing novel about employing jump cuts; what was revolutionary was their motivation and their place in the film's structure.

David Bordwell (1984) notes that despite the jump cut being one of most perceptible cuts, it has been neglected by film reviewers, critics, historians and theorists, at least until *A bout de souffle*. He claims that the sudden acknowledgement of the use of jump cuts as a stylistic device was the result of an increasing awareness of the auteur. However, this may have nothing to do with the rise of auteur criticism. Consider Pierre Lamorisse's *Le Ballon rouge* (1956), which contains a few jump cuts (see Salt 1992) or Louis Malle's *Le Feu follet* (1963; editor: Susanne Baron). Made only a few years after *A bout de souffle*, the latter contains extremely noticeable jump cuts which, in one particular sequence, slash Maurice Ronet's performance. During a party, Alain (Ronet), a clinically-depressed alcoholic, breaks down and launches into an incoherent monologue in front of the bemused guests. This monologue is riddled with jump cuts which are obtrusive, but neither absurd nor confusing. Contemporary film critics did not perceive these jump cuts as 'shoddy'. Philip French explains that Malle used this editing style with a specific purpose in mind: to harden Ronet's performance and 'to fine-tune and master a performance' (1993: 40). Even in 1963, these jump cuts were not remarked upon, despite auteur criticism being in full swing.

Film criticism, then, seems to have concentrated on *A bout de souffle* because of the nature of the jump cuts. Unlike other historical instances of the use of jump cuts (for example, in Méliès' films, to enable magical transformations; in Soviet montage as a realistic (see Bordwell 1984) and didactic strategy), Godard's use of jump cuts resists easy interpretation. The jump cuts in the aforementioned sequence in *Le Feu follet* can easily be interpreted: since they appear only in that sequence, they serve a purpose, namely to visually reinforce Alain's mental breakdown, his crumbling self-image, and thus ominously prefigure his suicide. On the other hand, the jump cuts in *A bout de souffle* aptly corroborate Bordwell's subsequent assertion that 'Godard's films invite interpretations but discourage, even defy analysis' (1985: 130). And what could be more provoking and challenging to film critics and theoreticians? Bordwell concludes that thanks to the emergence of auteur criticism and authorial readings, 'the way was paved for *A bout de souffle*: now, like other techniques, jump cuts could be *made to be seen*, to be read by viewers and critics in codifiable ways' (1984: 9). Yet, this is the crux of many techniques in *A bout de souffle*: they are far from being codifiable.

Barry Salt claims that the jump cuts in *A bout de souffle* were salient because they blatantly contradicted Godard's (among other *Cahiers* critics) critical opinions: 'One of the curiosities of the adoption of the jump cut by the Nouvelle Vague directors was that Truffaut and Godard had roundly abused Bardem and Berlanga's use of shock cuts and jump cuts when they were still film critics' (1992: 250). Contradictions of this type are a key characteristic of New Wave practices. The strict precepts established in 1954 by Truffaut in his article 'A Certain Tendency of French Cinema' would be flouted time and time again, not least by Truffaut himself.

Among the filmed titles, sentences and words in *A bout de souffle* is 'Vivre dangereusement jusqu'au bout'; literally, 'To live dangerously to the end'. A portion of it ('vre gereusement squ'au bout!') appears on a cinema poster and is the French translation of the title of Robert Aldrich's *Ten Seconds to Hell* (1959), starring Jack Palance. Michel walks past the poster after leaving Patricia on the Champs-Elysées. He does not stop or notice the poster, so engrossed is he in his newspaper. Our attention, however, is drawn to it: firstly, because the camera lingers on it, then pans swiftly right as Michel passes the poster from the left; secondly, a short, dramatic burst of music heightens its importance. We notice it not because it carries the narrative forward, but for its symbolic resonance. All the filmed words and titles in the film convey meaning, albeit sometimes merely poetic. On an obvious – too obvious? – level, this title seems to mirror Michel's reckless lifestyle, or one which he wishes to emulate: one influenced by American gangster or *noir* movies, at a remove from his real, deeply entrenched Gallic persona. However, the title also summarises the film's visual style: one which took unprecedented risks in the context of late 1950s French cinema. It is well known that Godard courted disaster with *A bout de souffle*. In fact, it is a miracle the film ever got made. Unlike François Truffaut or Claude Chabrol, Godard was penniless and the producer, Georges de Beauregard, accepted to finance him only on the grounds that Truffaut, who had won the Palme d'Or at Cannes for *Les Quatre Cents Coups* (1959), had written the treatment. Godard was barred from the studio system because of his lack of experience and the Éclair handheld camera was the only model that he could afford. Understandably, then, Godard was nervous about the enterprise but decided to take on the challenge of turning what appeared to be a recipe for disaster into a success.

I mention the genesis of the film only because it coloured its revolutionary editing style. There is a rumour surrounding the celebrated jump cuts: it is said that, after shooting, de Beauregard asked Godard to shorten the film by one hour. Partly because time was of the essence and partly because of his impatient nature, Godard literally took scissors to the footage and excised frames at random (see Villain 1991). This anecdote is attractive for it contributes to Godard's reputation as a filmic anarchist but, at the same time, the alleged randomness of the cutting seems apocryphal.

First of all, Godard, like another New Wave film-maker, Alain Resnais, was reasonably experienced in film editing. He had edited documentaries for Pierre Braunberger and travel films for the publisher Arthaud (see Marie 1990). In other words, Godard knew exactly what he was doing: the editing was deliberately 'shoddy'. Secondly, Godard is an 'auteur' in the New Wave sense of the term, i.e. a director who is involved in every stage of the film-making process. Although he employed an editor (Cécile Decugis) and an assistant editor (Lila Herman), the jump cuts are unambiguously his idea. As Andrew Sarris observes, 'the jump cuts, though not technically original, are Godard's personal signature, an index of his modernity' (quoted in Mussman 1968: 134). They are his stamp just like Godard's brief appearance as an informer. The jump cuts may also have been an 'homage' to the splicey prints which Godard would have often seen at the Cinémathèque.

The knee-jerk reaction to jarring jump cuts is generally to equate them with 'amateurism' but also 'unintentionality', namely a mistake that could not be put right. What probably shocked the spectators and reviewers of the 1960s was not so much the profusion of jump cuts as their blatant *deliberateness*. This seemed tantamount to vandalism and also a form of self-mutilation. Arguably, film editing is, to a certain extent, always destructive, far more so than the gentler deletions of literary pruning. Godard seems to have taken this mutilation to extremes and made it as evident as possible in certain sequences, thus highlighting the film's nihilistic streak as well as his own despair at that time.

However, on being told to shorten the film by one hour, Godard pragmatically made good the financial and temporal restrictions imposed on him. In other words, this was a style born of necessity as well as whim. This rhythmic expurgation is illustrated in the second sequence on the Route Nationale 7. After the stasis of the opening, this sequence conveys an impression of speed which mirrors the possible thrill of driving a stolen car across France. It also conveys Michel's impatience and restlessness. The infamous RN7 is one of the longest roads in France and the journey by car would have taken at least eight hours. Michel is of an impatient nature, so is Godard, and he is certainly not going to linger on a stretch of road that separates Michel from Paris and his goals: to get money off a friend and find Patricia. Instead of using dissolves to gently telescope the journey, four jump cuts in quick succession, which are both spatial and temporal, as Michel overtakes cars and lorries while singing Patricia's name, make the film jerk forward. The cuts have the effect of showing that Michel is racing to Paris at breakneck speed, barely pausing to admire the country-side or the hitch-hikers. He apocryphally quotes Bugatti: 'Cars are made for driving, not stopping', just as Godard could have said: 'Films are made to go forward, not stand still.'

Certain sequences are so accelerated as to become absurd. Consider a dialogue scene between Patricia and Michel as they drive through Paris; although we hear both characters, we only see Patricia, or rather the back of her head. This scene was originally much longer and shot in a more tradi-tional shot/reverse-shot manner. To achieve the jump cut effect, Godard literally tossed a coin to determine which interlocutor would be cut out. 'Fate' decided on Michel (see Godard 1980). The scene follows the medium long backward tracking shot of Patricia and Michel walking down a Paris street. Patricia remembers her appointment with Van Doude, a journalist, and a sullen Michel offers her a lift. As Michel drives from the Madeleine to the Champs-Elysées, he prattles on in a desultory manner, pointing out nice cars, telling Patricia he wants to sleep with her again. All the while, the camera records the back of Patricia's head (revealing part of her left profile) in medium close-up. The jump cuts begin, sporadically, when Patricia tries to explain her feelings for Michel. Finally, jump cuts and words coincide in a noticeably rhythmic way as Michel says: 'Hélas, hélas, hélas! J'aime une fille qui a une très jolie nuque – jump cut – de très jolis seins – jump cut – une très jolie voix – jump cut – de très jolis poignets – jump cut – un très

joli front – jump cut – de très jolis genoux mais qui est lâche. [Alas, alas, alas! I'm in love with a girl who has a very pretty neck, very pretty breasts, a very pretty voice, very pretty wrists, a very pretty forehead, very pretty knees, but who is a coward.]

In this second shot, or series of shots, Patricia's head remains in precisely the same position in the frame, but the light and background change. The continuity of the soundtrack softens the cuts. The rhythm is almost musical: a cut cues each enumeration of her charms, combined with a catchy tune which begins on the first jump cut of Michel's lines, which rhyme in their turn (héLAS – LAche). However, the poetry of this moment is overlaid with absurdity: Patricia's desultory sentences are ridiculed and Michel's list serves to fragment her, juxtaposing physical quartering with visual leaps in time and space. The impetus to cut may have been logical and practical, but the result is unsettling and modernist. It is also the negation of editing, by Godard's definition, since these cuts are not motivated by a glance: 'Cutting on a look is almost the definition of editing, its supreme ambition as well as its subjection to *mise-en-scène*' (1989: 78). Yet, because of the continuity of the soundtrack and the timing of the dialogue with the cuts, these jump cuts are softened, almost smooth. Agnès Guillemot, Godard's long-standing editor after *A bout de souffle*, rectifies a commonly-held view about Godard: 'Godard does not specialise in jump cuts, he specialises in cinema's correct pulse [*respiration*], which is not quite the same thing' (quoted in Jousse & Strauss 1991: 61). In other words, Godard was not being provocative but was trying to find a new and improved filmic rhythm.

If the slashing of Patricia seems absurd, nothing beats the sequence with the journalist Van Doude and Patricia in a Champs-Élysées café. This sequence begins 23 minutes into the film, after the sequence previously analysed. Michel has just dropped off Patricia outside a café on the Champs-Elysées. Patricia goes inside and takes an escalator to the first floor where she meets Van Doude. They sit face to face at a window table. He orders coffee, she orders nothing. He gives her a book, probably William Faulkner's *Wild Palms*. The shots leading up to the jump cuts are classical continuity editing: two-shots, shot/reverse-shot. Van Doude senses that Patricia is preoccupied by her possible pregnancy, her career prospects and her relationship with Michel. He decides to tell her a story to 'cheer her up'. While he recounts this anecdote, jump cuts pepper the flow of his story, accelerating towards the middle. In this shot, Van Doude is in medium close-up. He says: 'Alors je lui donne rendez-vous – jump cut – On déjeune ensemble. [*He lights a cigar*] Je voulais lui dire, "voilà, on est bons amis – jump cut – je trouve qu'on devrait coucher ensemble" – jump cut – pour voir, comme ça. – jump cut – Et je ne sais pas, ça m'est complètement sorti de la tête! – jump cut – [He laughs] [So I made a date for lunch together. I wanted to tell her, 'We're good friends, I think we should sleep together'. Just to see, that's all. I don't know why, but it went right out of my head!] Reverse-angle cut to Patricia who looks off into space then smiles to herself. Van Doude continues the story, but there are no more jump cuts.

For Dudley Andrew, the jump cuts are 'a pulse in the image and nothing more, actually working against the scene they exist within' (1987: 11), but another possible reaction to this series of jump cuts could easily be laughter. Certainly, the acting has something to do with it, but it is amusing mainly thanks to the editing that ruthlessly 'butchers' Van Doude's inane anecdote. The character of Van Doude is neutral until the jump cuts begin. Thereafter, he becomes a clownish and conceited figure and this also reflects Patricia's state of mind, *her* impatience with Van Doude, but also her fading concentration, wavering between his story and split seconds of inattention even though we are not privy to those moments, those flashes of thought. The rapid cuts may cause Van Doude to 'pulse' but they do not energise him, he remains seated, static (unlike the mercurial Michel); his anecdote is not particularly entertaining and I doubt that he succeeds in taking Patricia's mind off her preoccupations. When he finishes his story, Patricia does not laugh or respond but immediately changes the subject.

The jump cuts indicate Godard's impatience with, and lack of respect for, Van Doude, both the character and actor. It removes the actor's pacing which is remarkably insulting.[1] Note that Godard chose to hack away at Van Doude and not at Jean-Paul Belmondo elsewhere. As for the character, his story is silly, his delivery of it laughably pretentious, so Godard decides to chop bits out of him: he won't be missed. Michel may be churlish, but he is shown in a favourable light compared to Van Doude. Aesthetically, the jump cuts herald the video and the possibility of fast-forwarding (while retaining standard sound), except here it is the director who controls this function, not the viewer. Alternatively, it is reminiscent of a bad film print which hiccups and sputters especially at the end of a spool, of the sort of mediocre quality that Godard was probably accustomed to at the Cinémathèque.

Even nowadays when fast and hard cuts are quite usual in film, television, commercials and music videos, this extreme form of jump cutting is impossible to miss. The assertion that such cuts are now 'absolutely unnoticeable, so habituated have we become to the change' (Taylor 1973: 217) seems hard to believe.[2] What makes it so revolutionary is its obviously radical motivation. Whereas the jump cuts in early cinema, *Le Feu follet*, or music videos are intentional and there for a purpose, the jump cuts in *A bout de souffle* are also intentional but their purpose is unclear. In short, the jump cuts are not bewildering *visually*, but they are bewildering *conceptually*.

*Long takes: boredom and restlessness*

Long takes are easily recognised but not so easily defined. What exactly qualifies as a long take? They are seldom synonymous with sequence shots; more often than not, they appear in combination with some form of cutting within a sequence. The long take seems to fall into four categories:

- A take is 'long' if it obviously and substantially exceeds the average shot length of most films of that period/genre/national cinema/style, and so on.
- It is 'long' if it obviously and substantially exceeds the average shot length of the rest of the film.
- It is 'long' if it lasts beyond a certain point, because the shot is so complex and densely saturated with visual information that it requires more time to be assimilated.
- It is 'long' if it lasts beyond a certain point, namely the point at which the audience is able to assimilate the shot's information.

The long take is not just the absence of editing, for it generally relies upon the chain of cuts preceding and following it to validate its 'length'. In other words, relativity is the key to its definition.

André Bazin was a well-known champion of the long take, primarily because of its temporal 'realism' (1993: 64). However, some of the long takes in *A bout de souffle* are not exactly realistic, especially spatially. Long takes are not so much the *denial* of montage as its *complement*. *A bout de souffle*, with its alternation between montage and long takes, is a tribute to Orson Welles' *Citizen Kane*. As Brian Henderson has noted, montage and long takes are not antithetical, for both styles contain rhythm: 'In the long-take sequence, rhythm is achieved not by the lengths of the shots themselves (even where multiple), but rather *within* each shot, through movement – or lack of it – by camera, or both' (1976: 319). Henderson goes on to say that the intra-sequence cut disrupts the rhythm of the shot and affects the rhythm of the rest of the sequence.

Most of the long takes in *A bout de souffle* are by no means static. Nor are they what Bazin would label 'realistic', at least not spatially. Godard does not simply set down his camera and record whatever is before it. There are nine long takes (i.e. over a minute long) and several medium long takes (over thirty seconds long) in *A bout de souffle*.[3] Four of these long takes are circular, two are linear, and the three bedroom ones are static or quasi-static (camera movements used just to reframe).

If these long takes are addressed in the scholarship surrounding *A bout de souffle*, it is in opposition to the jump cuts, as if the latter were a yardstick for the length of takes in the film. Yet, in 1960, these long takes were almost as radical as the jump cuts. Technically, they were afforded by the Éclair handheld camera, normally relegated to documentaries or newsreels for their immediacy of response. For *A bout de souffle*, the director of photography Raoul Coutard was famously pushed or pulled around in a wheelchair (Agence Inter-Americana; Paris Street; *Herald Tribune* office; Swedish model's apartment) or a post-office mail cart (Champs-Élysées). The result is sometimes shaky but also remarkably elegant, beautiful and daring. The long takes also impart a feeling of restlessness and never-ending movement and, in contrast to the jump cuts, the technique allowed the actors to move and speak freely. This is particularly evident in the sequence set in the Swedish model's apartment.

Patricia has just denounced Michel to Inspector Vital. She returns to their hideout where she finds Michel sitting (for once!) listening to Mozart. In a high-angle shot containing two jump cuts, she gives him the milk and newspaper which he requested and he announces that they are leaving for Italy. Patricia tells him that she cannot go because she has just denounced him. As she explains her reasons, she walks slowly around the spacious open-plan loft, the camera constantly tracking with her. Then it is Michel's turn to speak; Patricia stops while he begins to pace around the room, again with the camera preceding him in a backward track.

The scene is striking for three reasons:

- its spatial verisimilitude
- its emphasis on the two characters' avoidance of eye-contact
- its overlapping dialogue

In contrast to the long takes on the Champs-Élysées, there is nothing to distract us from the characters, such as 'real' people or background movement. The flat is a sort of vacuum, furnished minimally, with just a few spotlights, pictures, objects and curtains. The lighting seems natural. The scene combines elements of both the declaration of love and of separation. Both are undoubtedly difficult to express and eye-contact would only exacerbate that difficulty.

Were this a classical Hollywood film, it would be easy to imagine either a shot/reverse-shot structure or a two-shot where both protagonists face the camera, standing stock still, one behind the other. Alternatively, if it were a comedy, the characters could be running around, but in medium long shot and with cuts to closer shots from time to time. Here, however, Patricia and Michel are not rushing about, even though they show distinct signs of restlessness, and the scene is far from funny – in fact there is something poignant in Patricia's physical movement as opposed to the stasis and sedentariness of her lifestyle and plans for the future (without Michel). Whereas Michel is often shown in movement, Patricia is often waiting (waiting for *Herald Tribune* customers, going nowhere, up and down, on the Champs-Elysées) or sitting (Champs-Elysées café; Orly airport). From the moment she discovers that Michel is wanted by the police, she begins to move (evading the detective who follows her after she has been to the *Herald Tribune* office). This reversal culminates here, with the long take capturing Michel's stasis and Patricia's restlessness, as if she had vampirised Michel of his energy (after his death, she also 'borrows' his habit of rubbing his lips with his thumb). In fact, he admits that he is tired, that he wants to sleep (to die?) and his final burst of vigour is undermined by his wounded back.

In terms of realism, it makes complete sense that Patricia and Michel saunter around rather than sit down in this moment of crisis. They behave as a typical couple who disagree and fail to communicate: they barely listen to one another and interrupt each other constantly. Instead of talking it out, they walk it off while remaining in the same space. The mobile camera avoids the theatrical pitfall of two people looking as if they are on stage; it allows the actors to fill their allocated space. Finally, the mobility also reflects the countdown to the imminent arrival of the police and mirrors the characters' racing minds. The take is not all that long: 2 minutes and 6 seconds, but seems to last much longer, especially in view of the amount of dialogue that is packed into it. The long, circular take, round and round, going nowhere, functions as an omen of death, a rejection of flight. Had the take been fragmented, this inevitability, this death wish, would not have been apparent.

Similarly, the long take in the Inter-Americana agency is appropriate to Michel's personality and situation. People do tend to pace about, especially if, like Michel, they are on edge and anxious to obtain their money. Aside from the opening shots and the bedroom sequence, Michel is in constant movement, either car-borne or on foot. John Orr has remarked upon Michel's restlessness: 'When he hotwires a car on the Marseilless waterfront and drives off to Paris ... we sense that he is doomed to perpetual motion. He is always in between places, people, lovers, so that every lover or city is a stepping stone to someone or somewhere else' (1993: 132). It consequently comes as no surprise that the film ends with Michel's death. After a long forward tracking shot which follows Michel running aimlessly, the film appositely closes in on a static close-up of the back of Patricia's head: movement is no longer possible since its source is no more. The circular long takes (the travel agency, the café, the studio) seem to symbolise Michel's choice of 'nothingness' over 'grief' which he articulates in the bedroom scene ('Grief is stupid; I'd choose nothingness. It's no better but grief is a compromise. It's all or nothing'). The circular movement acts like a spatial 'zero': in Paris, Michel seems to go round in circles rather than move forward.

Jean-Luc Douin, however, argues that the perpetual movement reflects the 'constant bustle and traffic of Paris' (1994: 121). This is very plausible, since the long takes all occur in Paris and mainly in public places. The scenes in Marseilles or on the RN7 are subjected to frequent cuts whereas the tracking shots on the Champs-Elysées or in other busy streets fully capture the hyperactivity of the city and reveal Godard's fondness for Paris, thereby complementing the affectionate – and unnecessary in terms of plot construction – shots of Parisian landmarks: Notre-Dame, the Arc de Triomphe, the Louvre, the Eiffel Tower. It is not just Michel and Patricia who are the focus of attention in the Paris street long take (after Michel has just mugged a man in a public toilet) but also the genuine passers-by, some of whom stare quizzically into the camera. Some long takes create irony and a dramatic intensity through a conflation of events. The travel agency or *Herald Tribune* office sequences, for instance, allow us to see pursued (Michel and Patricia respectively) and pursuer (Inspector Vital) in the same take.

It is also very probable that the long takes were a homage to Jean Renoir, Max Ophuls, William Wyler and Orson Welles, just as the jump cuts could be a tribute to Sergei Eisenstein. The New Wave was undoubtedly revolutionary but it was simultaneously indebted to the cinema of the past and it is no wonder that *A bout de souffle* is often described as a postmodernist film using a medley of styles. Just as the dialogue was novel with its mishmash of various languages, so the editing unabashedly mixed different styles within the confines of low-budget film-making, ranging from hard, rapid cuts to long, sinuous and graceful mobile shots, as if Godard was torn between the nervousness of American B-movies and the European tradition of a more contemplative approach. This melting-pot of styles would subsequently be adopted by Martin Scorsese *et al.* in the 1970s.

But ultimately, are we right to make the rigid distinction between montage and long takes? Is this polarisation not a little too forced? In a chapter on Hitchcock's *Under Capricorn* (1949), John Belton addresses a 'contradiction' in Hitchcock's work: his use – and advocacy – of both montage and the long take. Which of the two is the more 'Hitchcockian' technique? Belton admits that the question is absurd and argues that the long takes in both *Rope* (1948) and *Under Capricorn* are not in fact a negation of montage but 'its survival/transformation within a *mise-en-scène* aesthetic' (1983: 42). More precisely, Belton sides with André Bazin's assertion that *Rope* only *seems* revolutionary, and in fact, 'Hitchcock's long takes are, in effect, the equivalent of the classic shot breakdown [what Bazin called 'découpage'] of the 1930s' (1983: 42). Of course the key word in this context is the untranslatable 'découpage' which, as mentioned in the Introduction, clearly expresses *intention* rather than merely 'cutting'. The very fact that the word 'découpage' (literally: 'the cutting up') can still be used to describe a single long take and even a sequence-shot reveals that editing involves a lot more than physical cutting and splicing. Belton continues:

> Hitchcock's long takes consist of a succession of reframings and each reframing becomes a new shot. Though each 'new shot' is connected temporally and spatially to that which precedes and follows it, the continual reframing 'breaks down' the action of the entire shot into a series of successive actions which results, for Bazin, in a camouflaged analytic decoupage. (1983: 42)

Bazin contrasted Hitchcock's long takes with the 'découpage in depth' of Welles and Wyler which 'involves a breakdown of the action not by the film-maker but by the viewer' (Belton 1983: 42). But this distinction may also have a lot to do with the stasis/movement dichotomy of the long take. A mobile long take is likely to be more selective, more 'in control' than a static one. In fact, Belton draws a parallel between Hitchcock's decision to make *Rope* and *Under Capricorn* and his emancipation from David O. Selznick's interference as an on-off producer since *Rebecca* in 1940. The fact that most of the long takes in *A bout de souffle* are mobile indicate control, rather than the shoddiness and amateurishness denounced by contemporary critics. Although Godard's control was facilitated by light-weight handheld cameras instead of the heavy, cumbersome apparatus used by Hitchcock, the selectivity of the camera is nevertheless apparent. The choice to follow Michel rather than Patricia around the studio is tanta-mount to the choice to leave Patricia in the jump-cut car sequence. On the face of it, then, the alternation between montage and long takes may evoke the first-time director trying to find his stylistic feet, but in fact, the two seemingly contradictory styles complement each other well. The long takes bear Godard's signature just as much as the jump cuts.

Paradoxically, the long takes alleviate the potential tediousness of the action. It is difficult to imagine the travel agency sequence with conven-tional editing: it would be either very short or very dull: Michel standing at the counter, calmly waiting for his money and exchanging banalities with Tolmatchoff. Some scenes require ellipsis (for example at the begin-ning of the film, when Michel arrives in Paris), others are more exciting if drawn out. As James Price has argued, the contradictions in style create distanciation and alienation: 'The switching of mood sets up a kind of dialogue in the spectator, who finds himself questioning the reality of a character or scene, answering, then reframing the question in another fashion. Reframing his estimate of Godard himself, too; a Godard film is for the spectator an experience of continuous adjustment towards its author' (1965: 47).

The long takes, just as much as the jump cuts, bear the hallmark of the New Wave ethos which used location shooting and a lighter, less cumber-some camera. The long takes and the jump cuts both propel the film forward and demonstrate Godard's phobia for sluggishness and inertia. We have come a long way since the *Positif* critics' appraisal of the editing of *A bout de souffle*. Nevertheless, the film is still provocative and verging on experimental film-making. The editing sleight of hand masquerades as amateurishness and ignorance, and kamikaze risk-taking takes the guise of lackadaisical improvisation; *A bout de souffle* is certainly not what it seems. In terms of rhetoric, the editing would seem, at first glance, to be a string of filmic solecisms. However, whereas solecisms are seldom intentional but rather the result of sheer ignorance, this jaggedness and discontinuity were deliberate. Godard's conscious decision takes on a rhetoric of its own, one which uses apparent incompetence for effect. What was under attack, then, was not the abundance of so-called solecisms, but their rationale and Godard's choice to overstep a certain line of convention. Consequently, the style of *A bout de souffle* does not so much mirror Michel's tumultuous existence as provide a manifesto for Godard's idea of a new cinema which rejected the continuity rules of the Tradition of Quality. Just as Michel commits several 'actes gratuits', so Godard uses the jump cut for gratuitous effect, in theory to pare down the film, but in reality, to make a filmic and almost political statement. Using pre-existing editing styles, and giving them a new twist, Godard achieved the *tour de force* of making one of the first radically-edited French films to reach a mass audience and become a box-office hit. The 'shock' of *A bout de souffle*, despite elements of its cutting style being copied *ad nauseam*, has still not been totally assimilated, and probably never will.

# 3    STARS AND ACTORS

The film star, especially of the Hollywood variety, is a phenomenon that has generated a substantial amount of scholarship since the mid-1970s. Stars have been studied in various ways: as marketing strategies; as constructs; as signs. Different methodologies have been applied: the historical approach; audience research; and of course, textual analysis of the films and possible other material (out-takes, screen tests, and so on). What is interesting is that textual analysis focuses primarily on *mise-en-scène* and the profilmic, but more rarely on editing. The role of editing in displaying the star, however, has been acknowledged. Historically, the rise of the star system in Hollywood coincided with the first facial close-ups. But, at best, editing is hinted at through examples of *mise-en-scène*, for example in discussions of the distinction between stars as 'faces' (Greta Garbo) or 'bodies' (James Cagney, James Dean). Yet, the shift between shot scales via a cut or the timing of that cut is seldom deemed important. This chapter will attempt to demonstrate that, with regard to textual analysis, there is more to stardom and acting than *mise-en-scène*, and that editing has a discreet but significant part to play.

We already know that there exists a rhetoric of acting, which can be applied to film acting as well as the stage. After all, oratory is a perfor-mance of sorts, though one which discloses an awareness of the audi-ence. However, film acting is unique in so far as the actor's proximity to the camera may allow for more subtle gestures and greater interiority. In addition to the rhetoric of gestures and facial expressions is a rhetoric of the editing of acting. Broadly speaking, this rhetoric can be divided into two categories: fragmentation/stillness and completeness/movement. These are polarisations and are therefore rarely perfectly applicable but they can serve as guidelines. The dialectic is complicated by the definitions of 'fragmentation' and 'completeness': 'fragmentation', for instance, does not necessarily mean rapid cutting or jump cuts of an actor, but rather the number of camera set-ups used in a scene.

This chapter will take as its point of departure the significant editing differences in the treatment of actors. This will be underpinned by examples of star entrances, an examination of the changes in shot scale and the timing of close-ups, the patterns of reaction shots and how character actors are granted more spatial freedom than stars.

*Star entrances: putting on a show in public*

One of the key words to describe the star image is 'incompleteness'. John Ellis writes, '[The star image] offers only the face, only the voice, only the still photo, where cinema offers the synthesis of voice, body and motion' (1992: 93). However, cinema provides completeness only up to a point. When it does, it does so only in discrete morsels, the shots. Star entrances are a case in point: information about the star is disclosed in a tantalisingly – but expected – piecemeal way. The great compensation for this incompleteness is extraordinary closeness, unlike the imposed distance between theatre actor and audience.

Interestingly, interviews occasionally reveal that actors are aware of the power of editing which they may use to their advantage but film scholars seem largely uninterested.[1] In his memoirs, *When Do I Start?*, Karl Malden (1997) remembers how, for *I Confess* (1953), Hitchcock redressed the balance of close-ups of Malden and Montgomery Clift in the editing room, to Clift's great dismay. One of the striking aspects of film stardom is not so much the 'presence-absence' dichotomy as '*hyper*-presence-absence': the close-up is more than presence, it is an excessive, intimate presence in its myopic glory, one which terrified early cinema audiences but which is now visually fascinating and intended to be emotionally eloquent. What is more, we are at liberty to rudely stare since actors cannot see us. But to arrive at the close-up, a cut (or a series of cuts) is usually required.

As a general rule, star entrances are delayed and fragmented. There are exceptions, for instance Lana Turner's appearance in the very first shot of Douglas Sirk's *Imitation of Life* (1959). To a certain extent, the spectator expects this delay which is not particularly cinematic: it is a feature of theatre stars, and it is also a common narrative device found in literature. This convention heightens suspense, signals the end of a 'prologue' and a possible acceleration in the pace of the narrative. In some extreme cases, protagonists/stars make their appearance towards the end of the narrative: consider Harry Lime (Orson Welles) in Carol Reed's *The Third Man* (1949), or Colonel Kurtz (Marlon Brando) in Francis Ford Coppola's *Apocalypse Now* (1979), or indeed in the inspiration for the film, Joseph Conrad's novella *Heart of Darkness* (1899). Very often, also, stars are introduced through their distinctive voices or accents, and this is certainly true of Brando in both *The Godfather* (1972) and *Apocalypse Now*. In both, Brando's characteristic mumbling is heard before he is seen.

In his book on film editing, Edward Dmytryk entitles a chapter on acting and editing 'The Reaction is What Really Counts' (1984: 65–70). Film acting handbooks repeatedly advise aspiring actors to learn how to listen. Star acting does not necessarily involve much dialogue: Alain Delon, in Jean-Pierre Melville's *Le Samouraï* (1967), barely says more than fifty words in the entire film. Jane Wyman won an Academy Award in 1948 for *Johnny Belinda* (1948) without saying a single word. However, it is not the star's reaction to an event that really counts but the *other* characters' reactions to the star.

Paul Warren (1989) has based an entire book on this argument: he claims that Hollywood derives the power of its star system from continuity editing, and more specifically, from the reaction shot. He takes this further by maintaining that the essential ingredient in the making of a star is the reaction shots of other characters in the film. He cites the example of Marilyn Monroe whose entrances would repeatedly give rise to identical shot patterns, namely of characters reacting to her off-screen presence before culminating in Monroe's appearance, in glorious close-up. Although one could protest that this pattern is also in evidence in European cinema,

Warren's theory is certainly viable in so far as it emphasises the paramount importance of off-screen space in star entrances. In other words, reaction shots – glances towards off-screen space – are crucial because they trigger the spectator's curiosity of what lies beyond the frame. The ground for off-screen space will previously have been laid by media publicity, interviews and so on. But the cut from reaction to off-screen space to the discovery of the star is pivotal.

An exemplary star entrance is Rita Hayworth's in *Gilda* (1946), the quintessential Hayworth role. As is often the case, her entrance acts as a corollary to previous shots of characters (not necessarily male) looking off-screen. However, this gaze is *doubly* male in *Gilda*.

Rita Hayworth's entrance is delayed; she is introduced when the foundations of the narrative have been laid, 16 minutes into the film. As well as the title, there is some narrative build-up to prepare us for Gilda's appearance, but it is slight, based merely on what Ballin's butler tells Johnny. A wealthy casino owner, Ballin Mundsen (George Macready), rescues Johnny Farrell (Glenn Ford) from being mugged. A skilled gambler, Johnny had just won money in a casino. Ballin hires him to work in his casino and they become friends. On returning from a trip, Ballin tells Johnny that he has a surprise for him and introduces him to his new wife, Gilda, who we shall discover happens to be Johnny's former lover.

We first hear Gilda's voice humming to a record of 'Put the blame on Mame'. When Ballin asks if she is decent, there is a cut to Gilda which is almost on movement; she is in medium close-up and profile left, cut at the shoulder, throwing back her head, flicking her hair, as she softly answers, 'I'm always decent'. As she registers Johnny's presence, before Ballin has introduced him, her expression subtly and briefly hardens.

In this first shot, the frame remains empty for a split-second before Hayworth's glorious wavy hair, which was her trademark, flashes across the screen. The camera is still, but the cut is virtually on movement, prefiguring at once Gilda's restlessness and Hayworth's nimble-footedness. After all, Hayworth made her screen debut as a dancer, she was more a 'mover' than an immobile star such as Marlene Dietrich. The shot scale is too close to be ascribed to Ballin's or Johnny's viewpoints, but it is representative of their attention. This first brief shot of Hayworth, serves two functions:

in narrative terms, it highlights Gilda's eyes, which betray her previous acquaintance with Johnny, but the shot also reveals Rita Hayworth at her zenith, the star who primed audiences for Marilyn Monroe in the 1950s, whom *Life* baptised as their first 'Love Goddess' and who in 1947 was one of Hollywood's highest earners (Kobal 1972: 20–3). It also responds to the spectator's desire to be allowed into a star's proximity. Jackie Stacey, in her study of stars and female spectatorship, has noted that many female spectators vividly remember details of female stars' faces, for instance their eyebrows, lashes, teeth or hair, or other parts of their bodies: 'the perception of stars in terms of their body parts or facial features was, in part, made possible and encouraged through particular cinematic and representational forms' (1994: 210).

Her face is supplanted a few moments later by a long shot of her entire body and part of the room. This long take which captures her walking sinu-ously towards Johnny heralds the subsequent long shots employed in the 'show-stopping' (but also, paradoxically, very dramatic) dance sequences (the Montevideo nightclub, the 'Striptease'). Rita Hayworth, in *Gilda*, begins as a 'face' and ends as a 'body'. There is no progression from long shot to medium shot to close-up; quite the opposite.

As the scene develops, 'Gilda' takes over from 'Rita Hayworth': although both personae are juxtaposed, one persona tends to dominate the other, and 'Gilda' dominates the latter half of the scene. The first shots fulfil our expectation of Rita Hayworth and everything that she stood for: long mane, alluring smile, pin-up pose, glamorous clothes, and so on. However, her clothing in this scene is insubstantial and the framing of the second shot gives the illusion that she is naked. Editing plays a part in dis-playing clothes, especially in a film where a female star wears models by a well-known costume designer (such as Edith Head) or *couturier* (Hubert de Givenchy, Yves Saint Laurent, Jean-Paul Gaultier *et al.*), but it can also be used to frustrate and titillate the audience. An outfit can dictate a choice of shot scale and a cut can highlight a detail.

Thus, the generality that the continuity style of editing is subjugated to narrative drive is something of a fallacy: star entrances (especially when combined with star clothes) slow down the narrative. The takes are longer than necessary in narrative terms to allow us to appreciate the star, thus becoming little epiphanies, or alternatively, short enough to curtail our pleasure. Here, the first shot of Hayworth is frustratingly short, but it is emblematic of her movement. Luckily, this frustration is assuaged by the longer shot of Gilda which gives us plenty of time in which to admire the figure hinted at on the poster.

In other words, it is not just the choice of shot scale which announces the star, but the timing in the change of shot scale and the duration of the takes. Playing with the audience's desire and expectations (a star entrance should not be drawn out) and highlighting what characterises the star are what motivates not only the lighting, make-up and costumes, but also the cuts. This entrance is paradigmatic but also atypical in so far as the cut to Hayworth is almost on movement, whereas, generally, stars are immobile in their first shot.

Another interesting example is Bette Davis as Charlotte Vale/Miss Beauchamp in *Now, Voyager* (1942). At the time of the film's release, Bette Davis no longer needed any sort of introduction; her career as one of Hollywood's greatest film stars was firmly established. Most film spectators associated *Now, Voyager* more with its female star than its director, Irving Rapper.

As mentioned earlier, the appearance of major stars (especially female) in Hollywood films is often delayed. However, Bette Davis is introduced twice in *Now, Voyager* and this is entirely appropriate with one of the film's themes, namely identity. Her first entrance, however, is anomalous. As Andrew Britton has noted, the beginning 'elaborately [creates] the expectation of an "entrance" by Bette Davis which is then abruptly undermined' (quoted in Gledhill 1991: 205). It seems as though Davis' second appearance is the 'real' one.

Consider two sequences: Charlotte Vale's first entrance and Charlotte Vale as she descends a gangway during a cruise when she is mistaken for a certain 'Miss Beauchamp'. Both sequences introduce the star, but they also introduce two different and conflicting characters. The asymmetry is impeccable:

- Charlotte descending a staircase from left to right/'Miss Beauchamp' descending a gangway from right to left

- Interior/Exterior
- Dark flat shoes/Two-tone high-heeled shoes
- Dowdiness/Elegance
- Hesitation/Assertiveness
- No diegetic witnesses/A diegetic crowd of onlookers
- Off-screen voice/No off-screen voice
- No music/Music
- The camera remains on Charlotte's feet/The camera rises to 'Miss Beauchamp's' face

What is interesting in the first instance is how much information the editing and camera movements withhold and how this affects our knowledge of Charlotte and jettisons our expectations of Bette Davis.

Charlotte's first entrance occurs five minutes into the film. Her domi-neering mother (Gladys Cooper), her sister-in-law (Ilka Chase) and Dr Jaquith (Claude Rains) have already been introduced and they now await Charlotte. The butler is sent to inform Charlotte that her mother wants to see her downstairs. Our first glimpse of Charlotte will not be of her face, but a long take of a close-up of a pair of hands, working on a box, which soon drop their work. She then stubs out a cigarette in a saucer containing other cigarette butts and conceals the butts in a waste-paper basket.

Next, a slow wipe reveals a long-take, low-angle close-up of legs in flesh-coloured stockings and feet encased in black, flat, 'sensible' shoes descending a staircase. We can hear Mrs Vale's and Dr Jaquith's off-screen discussion about Charlotte. Mrs Vale calls her daughter 'my ugly duckling'. At this precise moment, the feet hesitate and recede a step. A few shots later, however, Charlotte does enter the drawing room, in long shot.

Before this final shot, we cannot be certain that the hands and feet belong to Charlotte; we merely infer it. We infer that it is the 'ugly duckling' to whom Mrs Vale is referring who backs away, recoiling from the harsh words. It is interesting to note that the screenplay (by Casey Robinson) and the film differ in one significant detail: in the screenplay, Charlotte's face is revealed in close-up as she descends the stairs 'by having the camera pan horizontally as Charlotte steps down more and more into shot'. In the film, her face is revealed only in the last shot, in long-shot, and it is barely recognisable as belonging to Bette Davis. This is not the 'usual' Bette Davis, not the groomed figure and made-up face that we remember and expect, at least if we remember *The Marked Woman* (1937) or *Dark Victory* (1939) rather than *The Old Maid* (1939). No close-up for Miss Davis – not yet.

After a spell at Dr Jaquith's clinic, Charlotte is advised to go on a cruise. Dr Jaquith prescribes a make-over and a healthy social life. There is some confusion on the passenger list which conveniently enables Charlotte to 'borrow' the identity of a certain 'Miss Beauchamp'.

In this scene, Charlotte is the last passenger to leave the cruise ship to board a tender and everyone is waiting for her. There is a small crowd in medium long-shot indulging in speculation and gossip about this mysterious lady. The music is nervous and rapid, then as the cruise manager suddenly looks off-screen right and hushes the passengers, there is a cut to the top of the gangway and an abrupt change in the music. In the first shot, a close-up reveals a pair of feet emerging at the top of the gangway. The feet are wearing elegant two-tone high-heeled shoes and pause for a few seconds. Two slow notes in the music seem to announce her presence; there is no other sound, the passengers are silent. The camera tilts up to her head, partly obscured by the brim of a stylish hat. We catch a quick glimpse of her eyes, free of spectacles, surveying the small crowd off-screen. Cut to a medium shot of 'Miss Beauchamp' walking down the gangway. Although we cannot see her eyes, her head is lowered and we surmise that she is looking at her feet, making sure she does not trip.

As in the first entrance, there is no establishing shot followed by a move from a medium shot to a medium close-up to a close-up, but quite the opposite. The close-up of Charlotte's eyes as she surveys the onlookers is a moment of great intimacy. We can sense her fears and misgivings. Similarly, the close shot of Charlotte's feet in the first introduction articulates her reaction to her mother's words, as well as leading us to believe that Charlotte is returning to her room. In the second shot, however, she becomes more public, and this echoes the stereotype of the star. Charlotte behaves as she imagines Miss Beauchamp would behave. She really does seem to take on the identity of a film star: she uses a pseudonym, the title 'Miss', is renowned for her tardiness and last but not least, conceals her eyes. This is the 'real' Bette Davis. The previous one was Bette Davis disguised as a frump. This strategy is repeated to similar effect with Audrey Hepburn in *Sabrina* (1954). Hepburn's first nondescript and lacklustre entrance as the chauffeur's daughter is later followed by a 'butterfly' entrance in full evening regalia which is witnessed by her father's employers no less.

If we compare the two scenes, the editing does not fragment Charlotte's body given that pans or tilts are used rather than cuts. Nevertheless, this technique rigidly controls the spectatorial gaze and knowledge. It also plays with our expectations regarding the star's appearance. In the first introduction, we are denied a close view of Charlotte's face. In the second introduction, which so closely mirrors the first, we are granted only the briefest of glimpses of her face which is rapidly superseded by the 'public' and 'distant' image mediated through the eyes of the onlookers. The cut from close-up to medium-shot articulates the move from character to personifying star, echoing the tension in Hollywood cinema between a conceivable character and our expectations of a star as well as the dichotomy between intimacy and distance/unapproachability which sum up the star. The first introduction was a little alienating – who do these hands and feet belong to? – but it would have been far more alienating had Charlotte's face been shown in close-up, for we would barely have recognised Davis.

It is almost impossible (and indeed not desirable) to divorce the three component parts of the star which Christine Gledhill (1991) has identified: the real person; the character; the star persona. The editing in *Now, Voyager* underlines this triad: Bette Davis playing Charlotte Vale playing Miss Beauchamp playing 'the Star' (Bette Davis?). It seems logical, then, to study the editing of star performances given the composite, fragmented aspect of the star image.

*A star is born*

We have seen examples of entrances of established stars, but can it be argued that editing can enable budding stars to bloom? *To Have and Have Not* (1945) by Howard Hawks was Lauren Bacall's first film. The story goes that Hawks' wife spotted the 19-year-old Betty Jean Perske on the cover of

*Harper's Bazaar* in 1943 and pointed her out to Hawks, who decided to cast her in the role of Marie Browning/'Slim' (which was the nickname he called his wife) in an adaptation of the Ernest Hemingway novel. As Bacall puts it in her autobiography, Hawks wanted to be her Svengali and changed her physical appearance, her walk and even her voice, which acquired deep, almost masculine tones.

An interesting sequence occurs at the beginning of the film, some ten minutes after Humphrey Bogart has already been introduced in the role of Harry Morgan. Harry and his alcoholic sidekick, Eddie (Walter Brennan), are based on the island of Martinique and crew a boat available for hire. He meets Frenchy (Marcel Dalio) who wants him to help some French resistants escape.

The manner in which Slim is introduced to both the audience and Harry is at once typical and original, or rather, it would have been typical if Bacall had already been a well-known star: her entrance is delayed and is similar to Bette Davis' entrance in *Now, Voyager*.

In effect, Bacall/Slim is introduced twice. As in *Now, Voyager*, the first shot of her cannot be said to be mediated by a diegetic audience. Frenchy is aware of her presence, but does not visibly register it, aside from a rapid glance, and this for two reasons: he already knows Slim and is not particularly interested in her (at least this is what we infer from the final shot in this sequence). To him, she is merely another guest in the hotel.

In this sequence, Frenchy insists on discussing the matter of the French resistants further in Harry's room. Just as Harry and Frenchy are about to enter the room, the door opposite opens and a young woman dressed in a suit comes out. At this point, only Frenchy sees her, Harry does not even turn around. The young woman is played by Bacall, but as she is recorded in long shot, it is difficult to recognise her. In the following shot, we are in Harry's room and we see Frenchy and Harry enter. A husky off-screen voice asks, 'Anybody got a match?' and Harry begins to turn round to the source of the voice: the off-screen door. At last, Bacall is revealed by a cut to Slim in medium long-shot, leaning against the door jamb. Harry, who is still in frame, throws her a box of matches. Some cross-cutting ensues, capturing Slim and Harry looking off-screen at each other. The shots become gradually closer, mirroring the characters' growing interest in one another. At one point in the scene, Frenchy is shown looking off-screen left, then off-screen right with a bemused and forlorn expression. Slim, having finally lit her cigarette, tosses the match away and throws the box of matches back to Harry.

If we were watching the film for the very first time in 1945, we might assume from the first shot that this woman is an extra like the women walking in the streets of Fort-de-France. With this in mind, the following shot takes us by surprise. Of course, the publicity surrounding this new starlet and her first film would have been pervasive and would have amply primed the contemporary audience, but they were probably not prepared for such an extraordinary voice. The spectator and Harry (who has his back turned to the door and does not notice Slim in the first shot) hear a disembodied voice, now easily recognisable as Bacall's. Slim is thus re-introduced, as it were, through her voice.

This shot very 'naturally' gives way to a shot of the source of the voice which visually re-establishes Slim's presence to the audience and Frenchy and establishes it for the first time to Harry. Slim, in the background, is in medium long-shot. Why not in medium shot or medium close-up? First, this shot establishes the size of the room and the distance between Slim and Harry. In this way, Harry is also visible (and so Bogart appears taller than Bacall when, in reality, he was shorter) and although we cannot see his eyes, we can be fairly certain, judging from his position, that he is looking at Slim (who is looking at him). (Frenchy is also present but not yet visible and even less noticed.) Furthermore, if Slim were in medium close-up, the suspense would be destroyed. Hawks is provoking our desire to see the owner of this fascinating voice more closely. Part of the attraction of film stars is that, on occasion, the spectator can expect to be granted a closer view of them, sometimes an overwhelmingly intimate view which fills the screen and the cinema. Hawks very seldom used close-ups but we can bank on an imminent medium close-up.

There follows a gradual progression from long shot to medium shot to medium close-up. The only words spoken are Slim's while she is in the room. Slim's and Harry's gazes register both antagonism (they could be two cowboys sizing each other up before drawing their guns) and attraction. Had the scene been in long shot, this tension would not have been so explicit. As it is, the scene does not require any physical proximity between the characters to be erotically charged, thanks to the crosscutting.

Aural and visual continuity is perfect which adds to the emotional force. Time has not been lengthened but thanks to the closer shots (which are also shorter takes), time appears to slow down, realistically giving credence to the cliché that desire makes time stand still. The crosscutting between Slim and Harry makes clear that the spectator is relegated to the position of bystander, like Frenchy. However, the shots of Slim also function as a means of revealing a new 'face' and a star-to-be, Hawks' creation. Of course, with hindsight, the scene in *To Have and Have Not* takes on additional meaning and mystique in the light of the blossoming off-screen romance between Bogart and Bacall. An analysis of the scenes featuring the two stars in *The Big Sleep* (1946) (some of which were added after shooting to make the film even more marketable), *Dark Passage* (1947) or *Key Largo* (1948) could be interesting in this respect. But also, given that the takes of Slim are slightly longer than those of Harry, it could be argued that Hawks was in love with Slim/Bacall as well. The shots of Harry record an almost comical response to what he sees, at first a little irritated by this intrusion, and then appreciative. It would be too facile to claim, as some feminist critics have done, that Harry does all the looking and Slim is merely an object of his look. The crosscutting of closer shots of Slim force us to notice *her* gaze, a very steady, almost intimidating, one. Bacall was not nicknamed 'The Look' for nothing.

In her article, 'Visual Pleasure and Narrative Cinema', Laura Mulvey claims that:

In *To Have and Have Not*, the film opens with the woman as object of the combined gaze of the spectator and all the male protagonists in the film. She is isolated, glamourous, on display, sexualised. (1975: 13)

However, the other male protagonist, poor Frenchy, is treated by the characters as if he did not exist; the only shot of him alone in the frame shows him looking at Slim but also at Harry, as if he were following a table-tennis match: he is the temporarily ignored character playing gooseberry, his gaze following both Harry and Slim. In any case, reaction shots are not necessarily male and male stars can be the object of female gazes. An excellent, though atypical, example is of Jean Gabin as Pépé in Julien Duvivier's *Pépé le Moko* (1936). Pépé/Gabin is singing on his roof garden (Gabin came from the music-hall and sang in many of his 1930s films) and an extraordinary montage sequence shows shots of (mostly) women in the Casbah listening or singing along with him. This also demonstrates that reaction shots do not necessarily need to be visual – meaning that reaction shots do not always depend on the *sight* of a character, and in this case Pépé is out of sight, on the roof (this said, there are also examples of *visual* female reaction shots to Gabin in *Pépé le Moko*).

The entrances of male stars are seldom as delayed as those of female stars. In *Pépé le Moko*, Jean Gabin appears in the second sequence; Humphrey Bogart in *To Have and Have Not* and John Wayne in *The Searchers* (1956) are introduced in the very first sequence. However, male stars certainly elicit reaction shots of other characters/actors as much as female stars. John Wayne's entrance in *The Searchers* is a case in point.

In 1956, *The Searchers* was marketed as a 'John Wayne picture' above a 'John Ford picture' and this was emphasised in the trailer and publicity. The audience would have known only too well that its star was John Wayne. The opening sequence amply plays on this expectation, brimming as it is with anticipatory and retrospective reaction shots and a silent and tantalisingly indistinguishable actor. It is important to stress the distinction between anticipatory and retrospective reaction shots. A series of anticipatory reaction shots gives the star immense build-up, whereas retrospective reaction shots can easily be confused with reactions to a line of dialogue or an action, not to the star *per se* at all. In *To Have and Have Not*, for instance, the reaction shot is both anticipatory and retrospective since Harry begins to look round in response to the sound of Bacall's voice ('Anybody got a match?') but it also anticipates the visual source of the voice.

The film opens with a black screen. A calm guitar melody by Max Steiner accompanies the sequence. A door opens inwards from right to left to reveal the sun-drenched grey and ochre landscape of Monument Valley and blue sky (thus foregrounding the other star of the movie – Technicolor). Standing on the threshold with her back to the camera is the backlit silhouette of a woman. The camera slowly tracks in, widening the aperture of the doorframe, a few seconds before the woman hesitantly advances out onto the stoop. A man on horseback can be seen in extreme long shot cantering towards the ranch. Cut to a reverse-angle medium-shot of the woman looking off-screen left. She raises her left arm as if to wave but instead shields her eyes from the sun's glare and seems to recognise the rider. Cut back to a point/object shot of the rider, slightly nearer than in the first shot. The rest of the sequence will continue this crosscutting pattern of reaction shots (from five other characters, including a dog) and shots of the rider. But even though the rider gradually comes closer, he is still backlit and indistinguishable – his stetson's brim almost completely obscures his eyes. We cannot yet recognise John Wayne's features but his swaggering gait gives him away. We will not hear his voice until the following sequence inside the ranch.

In this opening sequence, there are five reaction shots (showing the looks towards off-screen space) of six characters. The dialogue, such as it is, is very laconic. We only learn that the rider is called Ethan and is a member of the family. Judging by the characters' expressions, his visit was not expected but is a pleasant surprise. He is not instantly recognised by the family, probably because they have not seen him for a long time and he has changed or aged. Yet, they *assume* that it is Ethan (given that they all file out, fearless of potential danger), just as the audience *assumes* that this is John Wayne. The high number of reaction shots (almost half the sequence) consecrates Wayne as the film's main star from the outset. The editing makes up for the deliberate lack of information: Ethan/Wayne is backlit, the sun being behind him; he is on horseback and therefore his gait is not visible; he is silent and his facial expression cannot be seen; his body language is very restrained: he does not wave, for instance. Consequently, when he finally does walk towards the ranch, his gait and height can be seen as the equivalent of a close-up, and the climax of the sequence. Significantly, it is a comparatively long take given the shot's scarcity of visual or aural information. Yet, as we shall subsequently see, despite their physical activity, character actors differ from stars who are 'bodies' in one significant way: 'bodies' are the object of reaction shots, whereas character actors are not, or not to the same extent.

The European alternative

Paul Warren's argument is therefore certainly applicable to American mainstream cinema: the essential component of a star entrance in Hollywood
cinema is indeed the shots of other characters' reactions to that entrance,
and one could develop this further by establishing a distinction between
anticipatory and retrospective reaction shots. Anticipatory reaction shots

101

are even more emphatic because they create an even greater build-up, one which announces both the star and an important character in the narrative. But can the same be said for European mainstream cinema? Stars are not just a Hollywood phenomenon and it would be interesting to study the editing used to showcase stars of popular world cinema, for instance Bollywood, but we will concentrate on two of the biggest French box-office stars: Alain Delon and Jean-Paul Belmondo. A perfect example is *Borsalino* (1970) in which these two giants of the French screen co-starred. By the time of the film's release, both actors had reached respective peaks in their careers begun in the 1950s. Their acting styles, however, are very different. Delon's acting is restrained and sober, except in fight scenes where it becomes more physical. Belmondo, on the other hand, is more expansive, using broader gestures and speaking in a flamboyant and slightly camp manner.

*Borsalino* follows the adventures of two Marseille gangsters who start out vying for the same woman, Lola, but soon become friends and team up as partners in crime. Delon plays the part of Roch Siffredi who has just spent six months in prison. He is introduced as the film opens, during the credit sequence. We see him, in long shot, leaving the prison gates. The camera tracks back alongside him as he walks towards a street corner where two men are waiting for him with a car. There are no reaction shots and the take is quite short. Siffredi gets into the car which pulls away and a few shots later he gets out of the car in front of a cabaret, 'L'Ange Bleu'. Having swapped clothes with one of his acolytes, he is metamorphosed into a dapper gangster, all complete with a sharp black suit, a crisp white shirt and a black trilby. He enters the cabaret. Cut to a row of girls practising their routine with a dancing teacher. Siffredi can be seen in long shot descending the stairs into the room. But still no fragmentation and no reaction shots. At last, Delon is seen in close-up as the camera tracks in from a medium shot to his face. Siffredi questions the teacher about Lola and a brief burst of shot/reverse-shot comes into play. Siffredi extracts the information that Lola can be found at Adrien's café, and so the following sequence takes us to the café and introduces us to François Cappella (Belmondo) via a woman whom we will later learn is Lola. He is sitting at a table and clinching a deal, but here again, no fragmentation and no reaction shot since a mobile shot follows Lola to Cappella.

However, this pattern is about to change. If the star entrances have so far departed from Warren's Hollywood model, it emerges that these entrances were spurious. The 'real' entrances are about to happen, complete with reaction shots from one star to another. There is admittedly a retrospective (aural) reaction shot of Lola as Siffredi enters the café, noisily parting a beaded curtain. Lola is sitting alone at a table while Cappella, having dismissed his client, plays billiards in the next room. He is visible in long shot for the two rooms are partly separated by a frosted glass partition so that Lola sees Siffredi; Cappella does not register his presence and Siffredi is positioned in such a way that his view of Cappella is obscured by the partition. Siffredi quietly orders Lola to get her hat and coat – 'we're leaving'. There is no music.

Cappella and Siffredi do not face each other, but communicate to each other via Lola, as it were. They both give contradictory orders to Lola, Siffredi telling her to leave, Cappella ordering her to take her hat and coat off and sit down. Finally, Cappella and Siffredi confront each other thanks to an alternation of medium close-ups of each character looking off-screen at the other, beginning with Cappella's anticipatory reaction shot of Siffredi.

The rest of the sequence is taken up with a spectacular fight between Cappella and Siffredi reminiscent of a saloon brawl and which ends with the two men collapsing against one another, smiling, introducing each other and shaking hands before going home together to Lola's cooking. This confirms our suspicions that the two men do not know each other but immediately like each other. The fight is merely resorted to out of a sense of honour and duty and is possibly also a bonding ritual. What is particularly striking is the way in which the two stars' reaction shots bounce off one another and this resembles sequences expressing love at first sight. It is in fact remarkably similar to the to-and-fro movement of Bacall's and Bogart's looks in *To Have and Have Not*, with Delon playing the part of Bacall by entering Cappella's space and by being the object of the first anticipatory reaction shot of the film. However, in *To Have and Have Not* only Bogart had been introduced whereas here both Delon and Belmondo had already been introduced though without any sort of visual or vocal emphasis. In fine, the Hollywood model of the reaction shot could be applied to mainstream European cinema but with reservations: as *Borsalino* reveals, some takes are longer and refrain from fragmentation. Two-shots are frequent and close-ups are arrived at by camera movement rather than cuts.

In the above examples, the star is either silent or barely speaks – the emphasis is not placed on speech but on a new and pivotal character and his/her visual beauty or 'charisma'. A star entrance is characterised primarily by presence more than anything else, a presence which slows down the narrative. But what has this to do with editing? While comparisons between the cinema and the theatre are not always felicitous, it is worth considering star entrances in the theatre. The film star entrance is paradoxical in so far as it often introduces *absence* of movement (or reduced movement) – heightened by absence or scarcity of speech – in a moving medium. How would we know that this is the star, if we were shown a character striding across the screen in long shot? Yet, this is precisely how Jean Seberg is introduced in *A bout de souffle*: her entrance on the Champs-Elysées subverts the conventions of the classical Hollywood star entrance. A forward tracking shot records her in long shot, crossing the frame from right to left, with her back to the camera. All the traditional clues have been removed, bar two: Patricia has been granted a build-up through Michel's tirade on the road to Paris; secondly, a burst of music coincides with the cut to Seberg, and it is 'Patricia's theme', namely the melody which we will come to associate with her. The cut is on movement (Seberg striding into the frame from behind a parked car) but also from movement (Michel exiting the previous frame from the left). Seberg was reasonably well known in 1959, having just starred in Otto Preminger's *Bonjour Tristesse* (1957). Her distinctive cropped blonde hair and her American accent as she yells 'New York Herald Tribune!' are her only recognisable traits.

Tight close-ups are relatively rare in star entrances, but the spectator may remember a medium close-up as a close-up because of his/her heightened attention and because the face is of central interest in the frame. A close-up generally appears only once: a series of close-ups would destroy the effect of mild disruption or, alternatively, would be too disruptive. Moreover, the close-up of the star displays facial beauty: thus, in Bette Davis' first entrance in *Now, Voyager*, her face is shown only in long shot. Like the POV shot, the close-up should not be isolated as a cinematic phenomenon but seen as part of a series of shots, a cutting pattern which relies as much on tempo as on shot scale.

*Doing a lot extremely well: character actors and movement*

Character actors, also known as supporting players, specialise in second-ary roles which are often humorous. Their names are not always instantly recognisable, but their faces and/or their voices are. They tend to play similar roles in all their films. Examples from classical Hollywood cin-ema include Walter Brennan, Charles Coburn, Sydney Greenstreet, Hattie McDaniel and Thelma Ritter.

David Thomson has written that 'Stars sometimes just wait, reflect and dwell on themselves in close-ups. Character actors never get that time: they have to be busy' (1989: 33). If we cast our mind back to *Rear Window*, Thelma Ritter's performance is more than merely 'busy': it is positively hyperactive! From the moment she makes her appearance (which closely follows her off-screen chiding Brooklyn tones) in long shot, she barely stops talking while simultaneously going about her chores. Stella is as talkative as Jeff is quiet (not least because he either has a thermometer in his mouth or cannot get a word in) and as energetic as he is forcibly immobile. Ritter does just about everything she can in one room and does it with dexterity and professionalism.

Lev Kuleshov remarked that 'people performing organised, efficient work appear best on screen' (quoted in Levaco 1974: 99) and Hollywood seems to have endorsed this. Without going as far as to claim, Stepford-husband style, that watching women perform household chores is highly enjoyable, physical activity, no matter how mundane, is certainly mes-merising. But what is particularly noteworthy in this sequence is that Hitchcock refrains from 'interrupting' Ritter more than is necessary. I shall subsequently return to this idea of interruption in acting. In other words, Stella is shown displaying her nursing skills in some relatively long takes, compared to those of James Stewart.

In this sequence, Stella's dia/monologue is particularly verbose, yet I especially want to dwell on the interaction between her movements and the editing. Stella enters after Jeff has finished talking to his editor on the phone. Jeff then gives his plastered thigh a good scratch and becomes intrigued by Thorwald's rudeness to the sculptress. Jeff briefly acknowledges Stella's presence, though without great enthusiasm, as he is far more interested in the courtyard 'theatre'. Stella moves incessantly, she saunters briskly around the room, sticks a thermometer in Jeff's mouth, prepares the bed for the massage session while prattling on, and all this is recorded in comparatively long takes and medium long-shot. All this energy and movement continues until there is a shift in character focus when a jump cut to a closer shot of Jeff highlights his preoccupations as he says, 'She [Lisa] expects me to marry her'. The emphasis is now very squarely on Jeff. Stella will continue to be active in the rest of the sequence, perfectly going through what is probably the daily routine of putting away bottles and folding sheets and talking all the while, but she will be interrupted by frequent cuts back to Jeff listening or vainly trying to put forward his viewpoint.

The first few takes of Stella (not necessarily alone in the frame) getting on with her work are quite long – 36 seconds long on average – in contrast to the shots of Jeff alone – which average 4.5 seconds. But this is not the most striking aspect of the sequence. What is unusual is that despite Stella's non-stop chatter, Jeff barely looks at her. He looks sullen and it is only towards the end of the second shot that Jeff finally looks at her in apparent disbelief.

The absence of eye-line matches at the beginning of this sequence from Jeff's part is egregious; it is only later, when Stella advises Jeff on how to handle his love life that cuts to Jeff's reactions interrupt the flow of Stella's activities. But before that moment, Stella may as well be talking to herself. Yet Stella gets a lot of screen time which is not motivated by Jeff's gaze. Her movements, her wisecracks need no cues: Ritter is mesmerising *per se*. Nor are these long takes warranted by the content of the shots: there is nothing complex about them, nothing that requires more than a few seconds to be absorbed by the spectator. Indeed, they could be dispensed with altogether, since the narrative meat (Jeff's differences with Lisa) is revealed later.

As the film progresses, Ritter gradually becomes less of an 'actor' (in the literal sense of the term) and more of a 'reactor'. She takes a greater interest in the neighbours than on that first day and, as we saw in Chapter 1, she is granted a few point-of-view shots of her own.

Conversely, Grace Kelly loses her regal seemliness and becomes inordinately active towards the end of the film when she climbs the fire escape and acrobatically hoists herself into Thorwald's apartment. This certainly confers her with more humanity and ordinariness in Jeff's eyes and ours, but it does not lessen Kelly's star status. Unlike Ritter in the first sequence, Kelly's movements are interrupted by constant crosscutting to Jeff's and Stella's anxious reactions.

Another striking aspect of Ritter's introduction is her 'completeness'. Unlike the entrances of James Stewart and Grace Kelly, which both focus exclusively on their faces (and, in Kelly's case, this is cleverly preceded by a menacing shadow of her head), Ritter is in long shot. As we have seen, star entrances are usually fragmented, with the star being tantalisingly revealed to us in piecemeal fashion. Admittedly, Ritter's voice precedes her body, but that serves the narrative purpose of jolting Jeff out of his voyeurism, rather than intriguing us about the star persona.

*From star to character actor*

If uninterrupted movement and fewer cuts indicate the character actor as opposed to the star, conversely, the star can shed a certain degree of star value by appearing in sequences which deliberately avoid cuts and privilege physical activity, although this does depend on the type of activity. Two films, both avant-garde, both made in the same decade by women and considered feminist (though not by their directors) foreground an alternative treatment of the star: Marguerite Duras' *Nathalie Granger* (1972), with Jeanne Moreau and Chantal Akerman's *Jeanne Dielman, 23 Quai du Commerce, 1080 Bruxelles* (1975), starring Delphine Seyrig. In these films, two icons of French cinema relinquished their star status and embodied anti-stardom, if not a form of non-acting. In a documentary interview, Marguerite Duras claimed that she wanted Moreau 'because she knows how to clear a table' (*Duras filme*, by Jérôme Beaujour and Jean Mascolo, 1981).

Strange as it may seem, the very long and static takes of Jeanne Moreau and her co-star, Lucía Bosé, clearing the table, do prove Duras' point: not only is the scene fascinating (one of the high points of the film in fact) but Moreau somehow does it better, far more deftly and gracefully, than Bosé.

In a recent overview of Jeanne Moreau's career, Ginette Vincendeau (1998) has observed that her non-acting style in *Nathalie Granger* was a legacy of typical New Wave acting practices. Significantly, Moreau rose to fame in New Wave roles, such as *Ascenseur pour l'échafaud* (1957) and *Jules et Jim* (1962). In an essay on New Wave acting, Jean Collet examined the effect of New Wave trends in shooting and editing on acting. Jump cuts, for instance, may appear churlish in their fragmentation of the actor's delivery, but in fact, the scene would have been shot in one long take from a single set-up, thus avoiding interrupting the actor. Although the syncopated scene may jar on the audience, Collet argues that it was far smoother for the actor. He cites the celebrated sequence between Antoine Doinel (Jean-Pierre Léaud) and the off-screen psychologist in Truffaut's *Les Quatre Cents Coups* (1959) which smacks of improvisation. The psychologist was edited out because she was pregnant. However, unlike Godard, Truffaut did use dissolves to soften the jump cuts. But he did not change the camera set-ups to mask the jump cuts (see Gauteur 1962).

Similarly, Delphine Seyrig's housewifely chores in *Jeanne Dielman* (making *daube*, schnitzel, meatloaf, coffee, polishing shoes, making beds et cetera) are filmed in very long and static takes, many in real time, what feminist critics have termed 'women's time' although Akerman refuses this notion. Instead of being mind-numbingly tedious, these slices of life succeed in being compelling for us. Whereas Seyrig's roles in Alain Resnais' *Last Year at Marienbad* (1961) or Duras' *India Song* (1975) were of near-marmoreal stillness – a stillness redolent of the star – in *Jeanne Dielman*, she is generally very active.

It is necessary here to clarify the notion of 'activity' because editing does not treat all activity in the same way. Hollywood musicals, for example, fragment the spectacle, and this is patent in Busby Berkeley's extravaganzas, for instance *Gold Diggers of 1933* (1933) where the dance sequences become almost geometric. But in *Rear Window* or *Jeanne Dielman*, the activity is mundane and domestic and is rendered even more mundane by the avoidance of editing. But even an activity that is not usually perceived as mundane and which is seldom seen in its totality in main-stream cinema, namely sex, can also become mundane through avoidance of editing. Catherine Breillat's *Romance* (1999), unlike pornography, does not fragment the sexual act. Marie's (Caroline Ducey) sexual encounters are recorded in static ten-minute takes and are thus rendered meaning-less and banal. The sado-masochistic scenes in particular, although con-taining shorter takes, conjure up memories of television DIY or cooking programmes; they de-eroticise the activity by presenting it as 'a job well done', rather like Jeanne making meatloaf. And the little-known actress, Ducey, is certainly not transformed into a (porn) star but retains a certain amount of ordinariness, rather like Robert Bresson's famous 'models'. Significantly, *Romance* is another woman's film in which events are often recorded in real time, or 'woman's time'.

In 3 hours and 20 minutes, *Jeanne Dielman* chronicles three days in the life of a middle-class, middle-aged Belgian housewife who lives with her teenage son. While her son Sylvain is at school, she does the house-work, prepares meals and fits in a few hours of prostitution. Rather like Ritter in *Rear Window* or Moreau in *Nathalie Granger*, Seyrig does not have a diegetic audience: her son barely looks at her (he is more interested in his book, even at mealtimes) or when he does, his glances do not cue cuts to closer shots of Seyrig who remains in long shot or, at closest, in medium shot though sometimes truncated). We hardly see her clients, so she is not mediated through their eyes. Takes are very long, sometimes reaching ten minutes, and there is not a single camera movement in the film. Does Seyrig act in fact? As Laleen Jayamanne has observed, Seyrig performs only actions (movements which are not intended to provide meaning). She does not perform gestures, i.e. movements of any part of the body to illustrate an idea or convey feeling because this 'presupposes a sender and a receiver of a coded message' (1980: 99), and Jeanne does not have any receivers, any witnesses. There is no one to see her as a star. However, while it is correct to state that Jeanne, the *character*, does not perform gestures, Seyrig, the *actress*, does. Her performance was not improvised but was rigorously rehearsed. The dropping of the shoe brush or of the teaspoon on the third day was clearly intended to be read as startling and ominous.

*Jeanne Dielman* has been studied as a paragon of feminist counter-cinema which straddles the European and American traditions of the avant-
garde. The fixed position of the camera, combined with its unusual and
radical editing structure could be discussed at length. We will here focus
on only one aspect which pertains to this chapter, namely the treatment of
Delphine Seyrig, her literal and metaphorical displacement.

The editing is very noticeable in *Jeanne Dielman* for two reasons: long,
static takes draw attention to the passing of time and, by correlation, to the
presence of cuts. Secondly, it soon transpires that cuts (at least, in the first
100 minutes of the film) follow a strict and consistent pattern: they generally occur when Jeanne has completed a task and has moved off-screen,
leaving a few seconds of empty frame, but they either precede Jeanne
entering the room/frame in the adjacent shot or catch her *in medias res*.
When this system is subsequently disrupted (for instance when Jeanne
discovers the burned potatoes on the second day), a cut interrupts her
in mid-action while she is still in the frame and the kitchen. Thus, cuts
are always visible, whether 'ordered' or 'disordered'. As Ben Singer puts
it, regarding the 'ordered' cuts, 'We always know when a cut is about to
occur' (1989/90: 59).

Given this order/disorder dialectic, Akerman's treatment of Seyrig in
the editing is also polarised. At any rate, her framing of Seyrig goes against
the grain of conventional rules. In many long takes, Seyrig has her back
to the camera, for instance when she is shown doing the washing-up or
cleaning the bath-tub. At first, this strategy may appear cavalier towards
both Jeanne and Seyrig. Yet, Akerman maintains that 'the way I looked at
what was going on was a look of love and respect ... I *let* her live her life in
the middle of the frame' (quoted in Bergstrom 1977: 119). While it is true
that the static framing in *Jeanne Dielman* makes us constantly aware of off-
screen space, especially when Jeanne moves out of shot, and that the long
takes (and few set-ups) do not fragment Seyrig's 'performance', one may
be forgiven for feeling, with unease, that Jeanne/Seyrig is not the important element of the composition. It is unusual, after all, to let the camera
run on for five or six seconds after all human presence, let alone the main
actress, has vacated the frame and plunged it into darkness by switching
off the light. Nor is it common to begin a shot with an empty frame, empty,

that is, of human form. Now, this may indeed be construed as respectful. Ruth Perlmutter offers a striking simile to understand this mode of filming: she likens the camera to 'a child watching her mother's every movement, loving, but detached and unknowing, since forever external to her inner reality' (1979: 131). For if there are no cuts to closer shots of Seyrig, there *are* cuts to follow her around the flat or in the street, however mundane or predictable these movements may be. It is as if the camera cannot bear to be alone for too long: it needs human presence, preferably that of Jeanne. It is true, however, that the camera follows her into the bedroom with her client only on the third afternoon. But the camera is never placed in a space into which Jeanne will not enter, even if we do not actually see her. For instance, when Jeanne and Sylvain go out for their evening walk, there is a cut to the dark street: it is too dark to make out anyone, but we know, from the sound of their footsteps, that they are present.

Nevertheless, Seyrig can also be perceived as a displaced star playing the role of a *reified* woman, while the objects surrounding her become anthropomorphised or, at the very least, are given far more importance than in mainstream cinema. The real star of *Jeanne Dielman*, then, is the film set, this banal Brussels apartment with its legion of inanimate objects which confer meaning on Jeanne's existence. Let us not forget that the title of the film is not just a name, but also an *address*. In fact, Akerman confirms this: in an interview, she explains that the set and Jeanne were intended to be of equal importance in the film (see Champetier 1978).

The editing no more treats her as a star than the other characters in the film, yet the camera stares unrelentingly at the objects and furniture in each room, predating the fixity of the surveillance camera by at least a decade. Reverting to Akerman's remark, 'I *let* her live her life in the *middle* of the frame' (second emphasis mine), it soon becomes apparent that Jeanne/Seyrig is not always in the centre of the frame, rather the camera is positioned so as to achieve an optimum view of objects and furniture, even outside the apartment. Consider the differences between the first and second café sequence-shots. The first café sequence follows the sequence at the haberdashery section of the department store where, after purchasing a ball of wool, Jeanne exits screen right. Cut to a café interior. The camera faces two tables; the one on the left is perfectly centred in the frame. There is a vase on the left and plants line the window above the seat which faces the camera. The frame remains empty for two seconds, though from the moment of the cut, the off-screen sound of a door being opened and footsteps can be heard. Jeanne appears from screen left, smiles to someone off-screen right and sits on the seat, facing the camera in long shot, almost perfectly centred in the frame. She puts down her bags, removes her headscarf and folds it neatly. Jeanne is served a coffee which she drinks and pays for. She then leaves. The take is 3 minutes and 21 seconds long. On the following day, when Jeanne returns to the café, after an unsuccessful afternoon tracking down a button for her son's jacket, the cut occurs in exactly the same place and the camera set-up is identical but a woman is sitting in Jeanne's 'place'. Jeanne registers the woman's presence and this is indicated by a very slight hesitation as she stands on the threshold. She crosses the screen to sit on the far right, facing the camera. She puts down her bags. Coffee is served, Jeanne hastily drinks up, leaves coins on the table and leaves screen left. The frame remains empty of Jeanne for two seconds before cutting to Jeanne walking home. This take is 2 minutes and 50 seconds long. This second café take is shorter than the first precisely because Jeanne has spent less time than 'usual' (or so we assume) drinking her coffee. In the second café sequence, it is extraordinary that there is no cut to another set-up where Jeanne would be properly centred. This does not mean that the other customer upstages Jeanne, rather that Jeanne/Seyrig is literally displaced in favour of a preoccupation with spatial and formal perfection, a symmetrical configuration of objects in space. Moreover, as Jayne Loader has remarked, Akerman is much more likely to cut on objects: 'a table in one shot is balanced by a bowl in a shot adjacent to it. By cutting on lights, sounds and objects, Akerman emphasises the overpowering presence of the apartment' (1977: 10).

Ben Singer argues that, because objects are allowed to exist of themselves, and as a result of the fixed framing and distended time, we become more aware of the presence of objects, to the extent that our perception of them is sensual, not to say haptic, and 'this heightening of perception accounts to a large degree for the film's surprising pleasurability' (1989/90: 62). Objects take centre-stage which, by rights, should be the place of the star, and there ensues a shift of pleasure from admiring Seyrig to looking at the material world. Ultimately, this shift heralds the murderous ending: Jeanne's credo of 'a place for everything and everything in its place' (the washing-up brush, the shoe polish, the towel on the bed, and so on) is destroyed because Jeanne does not stay in her place and this eventually leads to chaos.

*Jeanne Dielman* is an example of unusual casting – the beautiful and elegant Seyrig in a housecoat – which was undoubtedly a counter-cinema choice on Akerman's part, but more importantly, Seyrig-the-star is superseded by Jeanne-the-character. Seyrig's trademarks are suppressed as much as possible: her characteristic deep and husky voice, which is powerful enough to remind us that it is Seyrig that we are watching, is infrequently heard; her languorous stillness is replaced by brisk precision. In other words, it is quite easy to forget that a star is playing the central role. Seyrig's attenuated star value is reinforced by the camera's patent avoidance of intimacy compounded by a total absence of cuts to closer shots. Seyrig may be easily recognisable but we nevertheless expect a close-up or at least a camera movement that would make her more accessible, more human, less mechanical.

From being strongly motivated by the audience's desire to follow characters' off-screen looks, to being content with following, albeit without as much eagerness, a mother-figure from one room to another, the fragmentation/completeness dialectic of the editing of actors does seem to contribute to star/character actor distinctions. While it would be incorrect to assert that the editing of film actors is encoded and abides by strict rules, it seems fair to argue that it relies heavily upon the triad of gazes: that of the camera, that of the characters at each other and that of the audience. However, the use of editing *alone* cannot determine a performance style or star status. For if a star was simply an actor who provokes many reaction shots, then Raymond Burr, Judith Evelyn and Georgine Darcy, who play the characters across the courtyard in *Rear Window*, would be A-list from the opening sequences alone. However, star status can be undermined by a scarcity or an absence of diegetic reactions or just presences, as in the extreme case of *Jeanne Dielman*. But the absence of typical strategies to highlight the star, for instance narrative build-up, an 'entrance', an establishing shot and so on, complement the absence of other norms which would be expected in mainstream film: frontal framing, a mobile camera, the elision of the mundane, and so on. It transpires that a crucial element in the establishment of the star is whether a character is perceived as a star *within* the diegesis. Bette Davis' first entrance in *Now, Voyager* is bogus for nobody sees her on the stairs except us. Her second entrance is a true star entrance because she has gained star status in the film. The example of Bacall in *To Have and Have Not*, however, demonstrates that star treatment can help to turn an unknown cover-girl into a sensation overnight.

Alfred Hitchcock famously asserted that 'the best screen actor is the man who can do nothing extremely well' (quoted in Gottlieb 1995: 257). This can certainly apply to the film star who is less physically active than the character actor, but whose performance is far more fragmented and interrupted. However, while the character actor is granted more freedom of movement, s/he is often recorded from a greater distance and in longer takes.

# CONCLUSION

The Introduction posed the semi-facetious question: does editing exist?'
The answer is 'no'. At least, not quite as we (think we) know it and certainly
not if it is isolated. Of course, editing does exist, but what has gradually
transpired from this study is that there are no hard and fast rules regarding
the expressiveness of film editing. The fact is that editing, like *mise-en-
scène*, is contextual. Consequently, much of this book does not focus
solely on editing, but also *mise-en-scène*, framing, sound, genre, history,
and acting.

The impossibility of isolating editing, of disentangling it from other
film-making aspects, partly answers the tacit and recurring question: why
has more attention not been paid to editing (especially since the advent of
sound)? Sound has detracted from and complicated editing even further,
and yet, despite the principal features of the technique of editing having
remained the same since the silent era (and by that I mean that decisions
still have to be made regarding selection, shot length and order), the presence of sound challenges certain assumptions about rhythm, for example.
The study of editing has gone by the wayside since the advent of sound,
and this can be explained to some extent by the fact that editing seems
more striking and more easily interpreted and conceptualised when it is
solely visual. Historically, it can also be explained by the unavailability, in
pre-film studies days, of video, which gave rise to the concrete difficulty of
closely analysing editing. Before film studies, only editors or film-makers

(such as Eisenstein) who had access to editing tables were able to theorise the technique.

We know that editing was primarily a practical means of erasing mistakes and allowing for spatial and temporal variety. We are also aware that, with regards to the montage/camera stasis and long take/deep-focus/camera movement dichotomies, or rather the 'hyperediting'/'avoidance-of-editing' polarisation, there is no such thing as 'better' or 'worse', but rather 'appropriate' and 'inappropriate'. What I hope to have revealed through this book is that although visibly different, these polarisations are not so dissimilar, and certainly not antithetical, in their intentionality. What really matters is how noticeable they are. The jump cuts in *A bout de souffle* and the long static takes in *Jeanne Dielman* are conscious strategies to draw the spectator's attention to the deliberate aspect of their editing. To the eye, cutting allows for greater speed and freedom than the more ponderous camera movement or drawn-out 'dead time'. Editing is not more expressive than avoidance of editing; it is expressive in different ways. Thus both editing and avoidance of editing involve selectivity: the choice of one shot over another, or of one take-length over another, is accreted to the choice to reframe at a particular moment or place the camera in a particular set-up.

This leads to the possibility of investigating editing in a new way: if a cut can be just as expressive, though in a different way, as the reframing of the camera, perhaps it would make more sense to approach editing as something broader, more far-reaching, and I am tempted to say, more three-dimensional, than merely as cuts which are not all that visible in the first place. In other words, to the question, 'where does *mise-en-scène* end and editing begin?' one could answer that since editing presupposes *mise-en-scène* in the fiction film, they are consequently bound to overlap. It is far more useful to juxtapose *mise-en-scène* and editing than to separate them. As a result, many sequence analyses do not immediately appear to address editing, but the inclusion of certain factors, such as framing or *mise-en-scène*, is germane and revealing, because most patterns of shooting presuppose editing.

This also explains why, when drawing out the expressiveness and the rhetoric of film editing, it is not sufficient to consider just a couple of shots;

the whole sequence, or at the very least, a series of shots, is necessary for a pattern to emerge. The case studies used here rely on a rhetoric of editing which is based on patterns of repetition (taken as a series of similar shots rather than identical shots) and/or alternation. Certainly not all editing is expressive: much of it serves the practical purpose of easing narration and comprehension. But expressive editing is rhetorical in the sense that it is intended to be seen and to be responded to, not just on a denotative, factual level, but on a figurative, connotative level as well. The existence of an editing rhetoric precludes the existence of so-called 'seamless' or 'invisible' editing. If editing is intended through its patterns, its rhythm or its timing to convey an emotion or affect, it has to be noticed to absorb our attention. Consequently, the whole argument of continuity editing being 'invisible' is challenged: continuity editing may well appear smooth, logical and linear in terms of narrative coherence, but as soon as editing becomes expressive, it also becomes visible. However, this does not mean that the rhetoric of editing, any more than the rhetoric of literature, can be broken down into a code or system but rather remains dependent on its context. Jump cuts on a character's face just before a line of dialogue, as in *Rear Window*, do not necessarily lead to character interiority but depend largely on the line of dialogue.

Last but not least, and this relates to the question of 'découpage' versus editing, we have seen that the distinctions between continuity editing and the art cinema 'alternative' are tenuous to say the least. In Hollywood cinema, whether Old or New, the 'découpage' or pre-shooting editing plan is implicit in the final cut. In other words, the motivations and goals of the editing are evident. They are far more opaque in an art film verging on the experimental, such as *A bout de souffle* or *Jeanne Dielman*.

Chapter 1, which mainly examined point-of-view editing and the struc-ture of repetition for emphasis in *Rear Window*, revealed that the study of editing broadens our awareness and knowledge of subjectivity and can yield an alternative interpretation of the film. Instead of an omniscient voyeur, Jeff is in fact a fallible stand-in for the director, metaphorically blind and ultimately losing control. What is particularly interesting about *Rear Window* is that Hitchcock claims to have made a silent movie, or rather 'a purely cinematic film' (Truffaut 1986: 319) in the mould of Soviet cinema, but in fact, the dialogue governs a large part of the editing. The aforementioned jump cuts are a case in point. Certainly, *Rear Window* may well be an example of classical Hollywood continuity editing but it is also striking in its emphatic point-of-view cutting which puts paid to the notion of 'seamlessness'. *Raging Bull* is, in many ways, the opposite of *Rear Window*: while *Rear Window* was partly 'silent' in its editing, *Raging Bull* uses sound in a novel way, with overlaps, and asserts its modernity predominantly through the dialectic between period *mise-en-scène* and innovative cutting techniques. It is expressive in so far as it is aware of its audience of film buffs. Montage and long takes with deep-focus photography are similar and complementary in their expressiveness. Nevertheless, our study revealed that the editing in New Hollywood cinema is not that far removed from classical norms.

Chapter 2, on *A bout de souffle*, contrasted hyperediting (the profusion of jump cuts) and the avoidance of editing (long, often mobile takes) which proved to be remarkably alike in their expressiveness of impatience and rhetoric – in this case, the rhetoric of attitude and of blatant deliberateness. *A bout de souffle* broke the rules of editing of 'le cinéma de papa', and its radical style of editing still jars to this day. It is still arduous to interpret and conceptualise.

Chapter 3 revealed to what extent a star can also be defined in terms of the number of (especially anticipatory) reaction shots he or she elicits from other characters in the film. Conversely, character actors' entrances can be seen to be more active, more complete and eliciting fewer reaction shots. Of course, this depends on the nature of their activity. The analysis of Bette Davis' second entrance in *Now, Voyager* shed new light on the aforementioned distinction between camera movement and cut; there is a tilt up to her head in close-up rather than a cut, but the effect is identical in as much as the camera, like a cut, rigidly controls the spectatorial gaze and aligns us with the character.

The study of editing is greatly amenable to further development. There is certainly more work to be done on this central aspect of film art, and an extensive world history of film editing (one which does not end in 1927 and which includes other major film industries, such as Bollywood, Chinese, and Japanese cinema) would be particularly welcome. This book prepares the ground for a comparison between the editing styles from similar genres and similar periods but also from different national cinemas to explore possible departures in editing rhetoric from the 'norm' of Hollywood. The relation between gender and editing could also be rewarding: to what extent is editing 'male' or 'female'? By that, I do not mean that editing could be more 'feminine' simply because the editor is a woman (which would be tantamount to saying that a large proportion of French films are 'feminine' since many editors in France are women), but rather to ask whether films directed by women appear more feminine in their 'découpage'. *Jeanne Dielman* is of course a woman's film, and its long takes could be seen to reflect 'women's time', but it would be useful to focus more on women's mainstream films rather than the avant-garde which is expressive in different ways. However, this would lead to the question, 'is there such a thing as mainstream women's cinema?' (see Butler 2002).

This book has demonstrated that a discussion of editing is not only possible, but also essential to a greater understanding of the ways in which films make meaning. As Eisenstein, Pudovkin and Kuleshov claimed, editing is indeed the foundation of film art, but it is a creative force in the sound film as well as the silents. Rather than narrowing down the subject of editing to reveal its rhetoric, this study has had to expand it to incorporate other filmic elements; it has had to address découpage in its 'lay-out' sense more than editing, découpage as the overarching design and vision. Ultimately, it is découpage rather than editing which needs to be addressed in film histories. In short, as Godard claimed, 'to speak of directing is automatically to speak, yet and again, of editing' (quoted in Mussman 1968: 48). The truth is that editing and *mise-en-scène* cannot, and should not, be separated.

## APPENDIX

*A: REAR WINDOW*

1. *(7")* *The composer and his musicians can be heard tuning up off-screen. Jeff has just been watching Lisa's 'silent movie' (she stands at the Thorwald bedroom window, facing Jeff's block, and shakes the late Mrs. Thorwald's handbag upside-down, with a disappointed expression on her face) with the help of his 'portable keyhole', the telephoto lens, which now rests on his lap. Jeff is in medium shot on the left of the screen, looking off-screen left. He turns his head round to the left as Stella comes in. The camera pulls back a little as she approaches his wheelchair from the left.*
   STELLA:        She said, ring Thorwald's 'phone the second you see him come back.
   JEFF *(grabbing the telephone on the right)*: I'll do it right now.
   *Stella looks off-screen front left.*
2. *(1")* *Thorwald's bedroom window, a point/object shot favouring Stella's POV. Lisa is rifling through some objects on the bed.*
   STELLA *(off)*:   Oh no, give her another minute.
3. *(4")* *Same as 1. Stella and Jeff both look off-screen left. Stella peers down.*
4. *(5")* *Eye-line match and Stella's probable point of view: Miss Lonelyhearts' silhouette can be seen behind the blinds in her living-room.*
   COMPOSER *(off)*: All right fellas, let's try it once from the beginning.
   STELLA *(off)*:    Miss Lonelyhearts... [*We cannot tell that something is amiss, but...*]
5. *(2")* *Same as 1. Stella looks concerned.*
   STELLA:        Oh, call the police! *(Jeff begins to dial).*
6. *(3")* *Same as 4. Miss Lonelyhearts sits down on the sofa next to a table. The musicians strike up the 'Lisa' tune off-screen, at the same time as Jeff is dialling, which adds quite a melodramatic touch to the shot.*
7. *(1")* *Same as 1.*
   JEFF *(to the operator)*: Give me the police.

8. (6") *Same as 4. Miss Lonelyhearts scoops a pile of pills on the table into her hand.*
   JEFF (*off*):      Sixth precinct. (*The 'Lisa' tune continues throughout the scene*).

9. (1") *Same as 1. Stella and Jeff suddenly look off-screen left which prepares up for a link between the music and the shot 11.*

10. (2") *Eye-line match and probable POV shot of the composer's studio window. He is at the piano with the musicians around him.*

11. (8") *Same as 4. Miss Lonelyhearts looks up and stands, slowly advancing towards the window.*
    STELLA (*off*):      Mr. Jefferies! The music's stopped her!

12. (6") *Longer shot comprising both Thorwald's and Miss Lonelyhearts' apartments as well as the landing windows. Lisa, in the Thorwald livingroom, is also seemingly captivated by the music and looks right, out of the window. Time seems to stand still for a moment; here the absence of fragmentation or camera movement is very effective for it forces us to 'cut' the shot and realise, with the same jolt that Stella and Jeff experience, that Thorwald is back. The landing window on the far left of the first floor allows us to see Thorwald returning. It is unlikely to be a POV shot which would focus more on either Lisa or Miss Lonelyhearts, since these two characters are the current focus of Jeff's and Stella's attention. We consequently absorb the danger more quickly than Jeff and Stella as it takes them both a few more seconds to react to Thorwald's arrival. Lisa does not appear to hear him and gleefully holds up a necklace for Jeff to see.*

13. (3") *Same as 1. Both Stella and Jeff are open-mouthed, in shock. Jeff, still holding onto the receiver, starts in his wheelchair, which gently clinks. Stella wrings her hands.*
    JEFF (*softly*):      Lisa!

14. (1") *Same as 12. Lisa moves left towards the front door just as Thorwald is about to enter his apartment.*

15. (2") *Jeff and Stella. The camera angle switches to a low-angle medium close-up of Jeff from his left arm, with Stella behind him, still standing. Both look intently off-screen left.*

16. (10") *Closer shot of two-and-a-half windows in Thorwald's apartment: landing, kitchen and a portion of the living-room. Thorwald is still on the landing, Lisa is in the kitchen. She must hear a noise for she suddenly turns round and scampers back into the bedroom, with the camera panning right to reframe her and excluding Thorwald and the kitchen. The camera stops when it frames both the bedroom and the right half of the living-room window. As Thorwald enters the apartment, the right-hand pane of the living-room window catches his reflection.*

17. (10") *Same as 15. Stella chews her right forefinger, wrings her hands and sways a little. Jeff, still looking off-screen left, sounds out of breath and stammers when speaking on the telephone.*
    JEFF:      Hello! Hello! Look, a … a man is assaulting a woman at 125 West Ninth Street, second floor, the r … rear!
    *A few moments later...*

18. (5") *Lisa and Thorwald. Same as 16. Lisa hands something over and gets up. Thorwald grabs her and the pair struggle.*

19. (3") *Jeff and Stella. Same as 15. Jeff seems to want to get up.*
    JEFF:      Oh, no!

20. (2") *Lisa and Thorwald. Same as 16. Lisa puts up a fight, turns her face to the win-*

*dow and calls.*
LISA:          Jeff!
21. (3") *Jeff and Stella. Same as 15. Jeff is visibly in agony, his features are contorted and he turns briefly to Stella.*
JEFF:          Oh, no!
LISA (*off*):   Jeff!
22. (3") *Lisa and Thorwald. Same as 16.*
LISA:          Jeff!
*Thorwald switches off the living-room light on the left, but they are still faintly visible in the bedroom light.*
23. (4") Same as 15.
JEFF (*softly*):  Lisa! Stella, what do I do?
24. (1") *Same as 16. The pair are still struggling.*
25. (4") *Same as 15. Jeff puts his hands around his neck and looks down. He cannot see very much but he can hear the scuffle, and his gesture is one of both powerlessness and a desire to hide, to cover his ears. He seems on the brink of tears.*
STELLA (off):  Here they come!
26. (3") *Longer shot of the Thorwald apartment, including the landing window. The caretaker and two policemen arrive on the landing. Thorwald stops manhandling Lisa, switches on the light and goes to the door.*
27. (1") *Return to the initial set-up of Stella and Jeff in medium-shot from the right. They both let out a visible and audible sigh of relief.*

*B: RAGING BULL*

1. (15") *A panning high-angle medium long-shot records Jake and Joey greeting friends and sitting down at their table. A priest approaches from the left and shakes hands with the men. An orchestra plays jazz on the left.*
2. (10") *Static medium close-up of Jake laughing. Joey, off-screen, jokingly asks the priest to bless the table. The priest's hands enter screen left and make the sign of the cross. Jake looks off-screen left, then centre left until his gaze is arrested.*
3. (4") *Eye-line match in slow-motion. Pan left and track forward towards dancing couples moving in the foreground, sporadically revealing a table in the background. Vickie is seated in the middle of a group of people, directly facing the camera. She does not appear to notice that she is being watched but is talking to the person on her right. Dressed in black, with her blonde hair lit from above, she stands out, haloed, from the others. A high-pitched piano melody coincides with the image, as if to underline her fantastic quality.*
4. (2") *Jake in static medium close-up as in shot 2. He appears transfixed.*
5. (4") *Second mobile shot in slow-motion of Vickie, now slightly closer, as if the camera has continued to advance in shot 4.*
6. (1") *Jake, same as 2. The fixity of eyeline remains unchanged.*
7. (5") *Slow track forward and slow-motion. Back to Vickie, still partly hidden behind the dancing couples in the foreground. Salvy approaches her from behind.*
8. (5") *Same as 2. Joey moves into the frame from the right to whisper in Jake's ear.*
JOEY (partly inaudibly): D'you see her? ... Over there.
JAKE (impatiently):    I saw her. I saw her.

9. (4") *Back to Vickie's table, shot from a slightly different angle, from the right. The shot is still mobile and in slow-motion. Vickie turns round left to speak to Salvy.*
10. (5") *Jake, same as 2. He looks slightly worried.*
11. (3") *Much closer shot of Vickie, still in slow-motion, getting up and turning round.*
12. (4") *Cut on movement, ellipsis and crossing of the axis: Jake, in medium long-shot, quickly enters screen left on what appears to be a landing. A rapid pan right follows him as he weaves his way through people. The distant sound of a commotion vies with the jazz tune.*
13. (2") *Retrospective POV shot. High-angle, slow-motion long shot of Vickie and Salvy's backs as they descend some stairs, followed by the other couple.*
14. (3") *Low-angle static reverse-angle medium close-up of Jake looking off-screen down right. He appears to be standing at the top of the stairs. He moves down and exits bottom screen right. The sound of angry shouting is heard off-screen.*
15. (4") *Frontal long shot in standard motion of Vickie reaching the bottom of the stairs. Pan left as the two couples walk towards a door on the left. A brawl is in full swing on the right.*
16. (4") *Same set-up but of Jake on the same landing and moving left with the camera panning to follow.*
17. (4") *Jump cut. Same as the last frame of shot 16 but further back to reveal the brawl as well as Jake as he goes through the door.*
18. (7") *Jake in medium shot, profile right. The camera has crossed the axis again and pans right to follow Jake as he goes down another flight of stairs on the right, leading to the main entrance. He looks over his shoulder at the brawl which has spilt out onto the landing. On the left of the frame, a man is attending to another who is bleeding. Jake opens the main door.*
19. (6") *Smooth continuity. Jake is shot in medium long-shot from outside, coming through the door. Static shot. He stands still and looks off-screen left. The music, which can only be non-diegetic, now changes radically to a drum and whistling melody. All diegetic sound stops until the bouncers emerge. Three people cross the screen from right to left, blotting him out momentarily.*
20. (4") *Eye-line match in slow-motion of Salvy behind the wheel of an open-top convertible in long-shot, Vickie and another man at his side, and another three people in the back. It could be a POV shot but the camera tracks forward slowly as the car pulls away to the left whereas Jake does not move from the entrance. The sound of the scuffle is still muted.*
21. (5") *Closer shot of Jake (medium shot) from the same angle. He looks right as two bouncers throw out some trouble-makers and the sound of the scuffle resumes.*

*APPENDIX C: A BOUT DE SOUFFLE*

1. *Long shot from the front passenger seat as Michel is about to overtake a lorry.*
   MICHEL:    Merde, la flicaille! [Shit, the cops!]
   *Accelerated version of Michel's theme begins.*
2. (½") *Long shot. Pan left of his car speeding past the lorry.*
3. (3") *Swish pan left, which matches shot 2, from inside the car, from the windscreen to the rear window to show the policemen overtaking the lorry.*
4. (4") *Jump cut. Still seen from the rear window, the policemen have overtaken the lorry but are further back. Swish pan right to Michel in the front seat.*

5. (2") *Very rapid pan right from the roadside as Michel's car overtakes another car screen left to right, matching the pan in shot 4.*
6. (1") *Long shot. Conflicting pan from right to left of the policeman speeding from right to left across the screen (so that it appears that they have changed direction).*
7. (5") *Long shot. Pan right of Michel pulling into a secluded track. He stops the car with a screech of tyres. The music stops.*
   MICHEL:     Oh! Le crocodile a sauté! [Oh! My clip's broken!]
   *He leans out of the passenger window and looks back at the road. Sound of a motorbike.*
8. (1") *Static long shot of one of the policemen driving by, from left to right, on the road.*
9. (5") *Static long shot of Michel lifting the bonnet. He peers inside the engine, then looks up at the road off-screen left. Sound of a motorbike.*
   MICHEL:     Piège à con! [What a booby trap!]
10. (1") *Eye-line match. Static long shot: the other motorcycle cop rides by in the same direction.*
11. (5") *Static shot. As in 9, Michel fiddles with the wires and looks up. Sound of a motorbike.*
12. (1") *As in 10. Eye-line match. The policeman turns off down the track.*
13. (4") *Medium long shot. Michel walks over to the open window on the passenger's side. He reaches inside for something that we infer is the gun.*
14. (4") *Extreme close-up.*
   POLICEMAN:     Ne bouge pas ou j'te brûle! [Don't move or I'll shoot!]
   *Tilt down beginning with Michel's hat (we see his right profile), down to his elbow –*
   14(b) – *pan right along his forearm, wrist and hand as he pulls back the trigger –*
   14(c) – *to an even bigger extreme close-up of the gun's chamber, panning right along its barrel. The sound of a gunshot.*
15. (2") *Medium long shot. The policeman topples backwards into the bushes.*
16. (14") *Extreme long shot. It is now dusk (the sun was still shining in shot 15) and a pan left follows Michel running across a field, without a jacket, a hat, or any belongings. Dramatic music swells. Fade to black.*

# GLOSSARY

*cut*
A visual transition created in editing in which one shot is instantaneously replaced on screen by another.

*continuity editing*
Editing that keeps the action flowing smoothly across shots and scenes without jarring visual inconsistencies. Editing is unobtrusive thanks to *eye-line matches* and *matches on action*.

*cross-cutting*
Cutting back and forth quickly between two or more interdependent scenes, which are happening simultaneously (e.g. the end of *The Godfather* (Coppola, 1972) which alternates acts of violence with a baptism).

*dissolve*
A gradual scene transition which overlaps the end of one shot into the beginning of the next.

*errors of continuity*
Disruptions in the flow of a scene, such as a failure to match action or the placement of props across shots. See also *180° rule*.

*establishing shot*
Usually an extreme long shot or a long shot used near the beginning of a scene to establish the space where the action will unfold.

*eye-line match*
The matching of eye-lines between two or more characters across two shots. For example, in a dialogue scene, character A looks off-screen right in shot 1, and character B looks off-screen left in shot 2. Shot 2 fills in the off-screen space of shot 1. This establishes a relationship of proximity and continuity.

*fade*
A visual transition between shots or scenes that appears on screen as a brief interval with no picture. The editor fades one shot to black (usually) and then fades in the next. Often used to indicate a change in time and place.

*final cut*
The finished edit of a film, approved by the director and the producer. This is what the audience sees.

*iris*
A fade-in or -out in which the image appears or disappears as an opening or closing circle. Common during the silent era.

*jump cut*
A cut which breaks the continuity by leaving out parts of the action (see Chapter 1).

*matched cut* or *match on action*
A cut joining two shots whose movements within the frame match, helping to establish strong continuity of action. In shot 1, character A raises his arm and waves off-screen right. In shot 2, Character B raises her arm and waves off-screen left and starts running to the left.

*montage*
Scenes whose emotional impact and visual design are achieved through the editing together of many brief shots. Montage may expand or contract time and/or space. The shower scene in *Psycho* is an example of montage editing which expands and magnifies the action.

*180° rule*
A common convention in Western *continuity editing* which stipulates that the camera should not cross the 180° line or axis of action. This imaginary line is determined by the action. It can occur between two people conversing or on the trajectory of a person walking. If the camera crosses this line abruptly, for example if the camera position changes between shots or takes, the viewer may feel momentarily disorientated. For instance, in a typical *shot/reverse-shot* exchange, character A looks off-screen right in shot 1 while character B looks off-screen left in shot 2. However, if the camera were to cross the 180° line in shot 2, character B would be looking off-screen right. Thus, the two characters would appear to look in the *same* direction, rather than *at* each other, which would be misleading.

*optical effect*
Transitional device such as a fade, dissolve, iris and wipe. It can act as a way of avoiding an abrupt ending to a sequence and a potentially disorientating shift to another space and/or time.

*sequence shot* or *plan-séquence*
A long and usually complex take that extends for an entire scene or sequence. It is composed of only one shot with no editing.

*shot scale*
The distance between the camera and the subject. The closest shot scale is an extreme close-up (ECU); at the other end of the spectrum is the extreme long-shot (ELS) which can sometimes be identical to an establishing shot which sets the scene.

*shot/reverse-shot*
Usually used for conversation scenes, this technique alternates over-the-shoulder shots showing each character speaking.

*30° rule*
In continuity editing, the camera set-up must move by more than 30° from one shot to the next, or the result will be a *jump cut*.

*two-shot*
Shot framing two people.

*wipe*
Visible on screen as a bar travelling across the frame pushing one shot off and pulling the next shot into place. Rarely used in contemporary film, but common in films of the 1930s and 1940s.

# NOTES

## INTRODUCTION

1     V.F. Perkins has suggested that the term could be translated as 'layout', which conveys the visual sense of 'découpage' (in conversation with the author).

2     For instance, in Louis Gianetti & Scott Eyman (1996) *Flashback: A Brief History of Film*. Englewood Cliffs, New Jersey: Prentice Hall. Third Edition. See also David Bordwell's (1997) *On the History of Film Style*. Cambridge, Mass.: Harvard University Press, which only briefly mentions continuity editing (as well as the obligatory investigation of montage in silent films).

3     This is the case in Gerald Mast (1986) *A Short History of the Movies*, Fourth Edition. London: Collier Macmillan; Jack C. Ellis (1995) *A History of Film*, Fourth Edition. London: Allyn and Bacon.

4     For instance, Ralph Rosenblum (1979) *When the Shooting Stops, the Cutting Begins: An Editor's Story*. New York: Penguin.

5     Vincent Lo Brutto (1991) *Selected Takes: Film Editors on Editing*. Westport, Connecticut: Praeger; Gabriella Oldham (1992) *First Cut: Conversations with Film Editors*. Berkeley: University of California Press.

## CHAPTER ONE

1     In this discussion I have divided the film into five parts: Wednesday, Thursday, Friday, Saturday and Epilogue.

2     This expression ('*point d'écoute*') was first used by Claude Bailblé in *Cahiers du Cinéma*, 292, 23 and has been quoted by Michel Chion (1985) in *Le Son au cinéma*. Paris: Éditions de l'Étoile/Cahiers du Cinéma, 51.

3   They appear in *Mean Streets* (1973) (religious icons), and *The Color of Money* (1986) (cues, balls, chalk). In *Raging Bull:* the bell in the ring, round cards, a light bulb, light switch, bottle necks, half a telephone, coat hangers...

4   Schoonmaker also pointed out that 'when you use flashbulbs, you can cut anywhere and use jump cuts'. Thelma Schoonmaker interviewed by Ian Christie, National Film Theatre Masterclass, 23 November 1997.

## CHAPTER TWO

1   This lack of respect for actors is confirmed by Godard in an interview: 'My relationships with actors are very hostile. I don't speak to them ... They don't have a destiny and they know it. They are always conscious of their mutilation. The gap between the creator and the actor is the same as the gap between being and having. An actor cannot *be.*' Interview with Sylvain Regard (1966) 'La Vie moderne', *Le Nouvel Observateur*, 100, October 12–18, 56, quoted in Julia Lesage (1976) *The Films of Jean-Luc Godard and their Use of Brechtian Drama*. Ann Arbor: University Microfilms, 32. My translation.

2   See also Susan Sontag (1968) 'Going to the Movies: Godard', *The Partisan Review*, 2, Spring, 290: 'The once obtrusive cutting and the oddities of the handheld camera are almost invisible, so widely imitated are these techniques now'.

3   The long takes are: The Champs-Elysées (Michel and Patricia); two of the Agence Inter-Americana (Michel and Tolmatchoff; the detectives); a Paris Street (Michel and Patricia); three of the bedroom (Michel and Patricia); the *Herald Tribune* office (Patricia and Inspector Vital); the Swedish model's apartment, rue Campagne-Première (Patricia and Michel).

## CHAPTER THREE

1   The producer of *Sliver* (1993), Robert Evans, claims that Sharon Stone manipulated her screen image via editing: 'Stone was less effective in shots that included other actors than in her close-ups – thereby forcing the editors to use those in the final cut and pushing Baldwin out of her scenes.' Jess Cagle (1993) 'Many a slip...', *Empire*, 51, September, 96. Robert De Niro, however, believes that the actor is subordinated to the director's decisions: 'You can disagree, you can try it your way, their way, ultimately they edit it and it's their film.' From a *Guardian* lecture reprinted in *Three Sixty Degrees: British Film Institute News* (1985), May, 10–11, quoted in Barry King (1991) 'Articulating Stardom', in Jeremy G. Butler (ed.) *Star Texts: Image and Performance in Film and* Television. Detroit: Wayne State University Press, 143.

# FILMOGRAPHY

*A bout de souffle* (Jean-Luc Godard, 1959, Fr., ed. Cécile Decugis)
*All the King's Men* (Robert Rossen, 1949, US, ed. Robert Parrish)
*L'Année dernière à Marienbad* (Alain Resnais, 1961, Fr., eds. Jasmine Chasney and Henri Colpi)
*Apocalypse Now* (Francis Ford Coppola, 1979, US, eds. Lisa Fruchtman, Gerald B. Greenberg, Richard Marks, Walter Murch)
*Ascenseur pour l'échafaud* (Louis Malle, 1957, Fr., ed. Léonide Azar)
*Le Ballon rouge* (Pierre Lamorrisse, 1956, Fr., ed. Pierre Gillette)
*Battleship Potemkin* (Sergei Eisenstein, 1925, USSR, ed. Sergei Eisenstein)
*The Big Sleep* (Howard Hawks, 1946, US, ed. Christian Nyby)
*The Birds* (Alfred Hitchcock, 1964, US, ed. George Tomasini)
*Blade Runner* (Ridley Scott, 1982, US, ed. Terry Rawlings)
*Bonjour Tristesse* (Otto Preminger, 1957, UK, ed. Helga Cranston)
*Bonnie and Clyde* (Arthur Penn, 1967, US, ed. Dede Allen)
*Borsalino* (Jacques Deray, 1970, Fr., ed. Paul Cayatte)
*Les Carabiniers* (Jean-Luc Godard, Fr., 1963, ed. Agnès Guillemot)
*Citizen Kane* (Orson Welles, 1941, US, ed. Robert Wise)
*Cléo de cinq à sept* (Agnès Varda, 1961, Fr., ed. Jeanne Verneau)
*Dark Passage* (Delmer Daves, 1947, US, ed. David Weisbart)
*Dark Victory* (Edmund Goulding, 1939, US, ed. William Holmes)
*Les Deux Anglaises et le continent* (François Truffaut, 1971, Fr., ed. Yann Dedet)
*Le Feu follet* (Louis Malle, 1963, Fr., ed. Susanne Baron)
*Gilda* (Charles Vidor, 1946, US, ed. Charles Nelson)
*The Godfather* (Francis Ford Coppola, 1972, US, eds. Marc Laub, Barbara Marks, William Reynolds, Murray Solomon, Peter Zinner)
*Gold Diggers of 1933* (Mervyn Le Roy, 1933, US, ed. George Amy)
*GoodFellas* (Martin Scorsese, 1990, US, ed. Thelma Schoonmaker)
*The Harder they Fall* (Mark Robson, US, 1956, ed. Jerome Thoms)
*Hana-Bi* (Takeshi Kitano, 1997, Japan, eds. Takeshi Kitano and Ota Yoshinori)
*Hiroshima mon amour* (Alain Resnais, 1959, Fr., eds. Jasmine Chasney, Henri Colpi and Anne Sarraute)

*His Girl Friday* (Howard Hawks, 1939, US, ed. Gene Havlick)
*I Confess* (Alfred Hitchcock, 1953, US, ed. Rudi Fehr)
*Imitation of Life* (Douglas Sirk, 1959, US, ed. Milton Carruth)
*In Harm's Way* (Otto Preminger, 1965, US, ed. George Tomasini)
*India Song* (Marguerite Duras, 1975, Fr., ed. Solange Leprince)
*Jeanne Dielman, 23 Quai du Commerce, 1080 Bruxelles* (Chantal Akerman, 1975, Belgium, ed. Patricia Canino)
*Johnny Belinda* (Jean Negulesco, 1948, US, ed. David Weisbart)
*Jules et Jim* (François Truffaut, 1962, Fr., ed. Claudine Bouché)
*Key Largo* (John Huston, 1948, US, ed. Rudi Fehr)
*The Lady from Shanghai* (Orson Welles, 1948, US, ed. Viola Lawrence)
*The Lady in the Lake* (Robert Montgomery, 1946, US, ed. Gene Ruggiero)
*The Magnificent Ambersons* (Orson Welles, 1942, US, ed. Robert Wise)
*The Man Who Knew Too Much* (Alfred Hitchcock, 1956, US, ed. George Tomasini)
*The Marked Woman* (Lloyd Bacon, 1937, US, ed. Jack Killifer)
*Marnie* (Alfred Hitchcock, 1963, US, ed. George Tomasini)
*A Matter of Life and Death* (Michael Powell and Emeric Pressburger, 1946, US, ed. Reginald Mills)
*Mean Streets* (Martin Scorsese, 1973, US, ed. Sidney Levin)
*Le Mépris* (Jean-Luc Godard, 1963, Fr., ed. Agnès Guillemot)
*The Misfits* (John Huston, 1961, US, ed. George Tomasini)
*Nathalie Granger* (Marguerite Duras, 1972, Fr., editor uncredited)
*North by Northwest* (Alfred Hitchcock, 1959, US, ed. George Tomasini)
*Notorious* (Alfred Hitchcock, 1946, US, ed. Theron Warth)
*La Notte* (Michelangelo Antonioni, 1960, It., ed. Eraldo Da Roma)
*Now, Voyager* (Irving Rapper, 1942, US, ed. Warren Low)
*The Old Maid* (Edmund Goulding, 1939, US, ed. George Amy)
*Pépé le Moko* (Julien Duvivier, 1936, Fr., ed. Marguerite Beaugé)
*Pierrot le fou* (Jean-Luc Godard, 1966, Fr., ed. Françoise Colin)
*Psycho* (Alfred Hitchcock, 1960, US, ed. George Tomasini)
*Les Quatre Cents Coups* (François Truffaut, 1959, Fr., ed. Agnès Guillemot)
*La Règle du jeu* (Jean Renoir, 1939, Fr., ed. Marthe Huguet and Marguerite Renoir)
*Romance* (Catherine Breillat, 1999, Fr., ed. Agnès Guillemot)
*A Room With a View* (James Ivory, 1985, UK, ed. Humphrey Dixon)
*Rope* (Alfred Hitchcock, 1948, US, ed. William H. Ziegler)
*Sabrina* (Billy Wilder, 1954, US, ed. Arthur P. Schmidt)
*Le Samouraï* (Jean-Pierre Melville, 1967, Fr., eds. Monique Bonnot and Yolande Maurette)
*The Searchers* (John Ford, 1956, US, ed. Jack Murray)
*The Set-Up* (Robert Wise, 1949, US, ed. Roland Gross)
*The Silence of the Lambs* (Jonathan Demme, 1991, US, ed. Craig McKay)
*Stalag 17* (Billy Wilder, 1953, US, ed. George Tomasini)
*Ten Seconds to Hell* (Robert Aldrich, 1959, US, eds. James Needs. and Henry Richardson)
*The Third Man* (Carol Reed, 1949, US, ed. Oswald Hafenrichter)
*To Catch a Thief* (Alfred Hitchcock, 1955, US, ed. George Tomasini)
*To Have and Have Not* (Howard Hawks, 1945, US, ed. Christian Nyby)
*Under Capricorn* (Alfred Hitchcock, 1949, US, ed. A.S. Bates)
*Vertigo* (Alfred Hitchcock, 1958, US, ed. George Tomasini)
*The Wrong Man* (Alfred Hitchcock, 1957, US, ed. George Tomasini)

# BIBLIOGRAPHY

The bibliography lists works cited in the text and is also designed to point to useful further reading. The 'essential reading' list highlights works considered to be of particular importance to the understanding of film editing, although many valuable contributions are also to be found under 'secondary reading'.

ESSENTIAL READING

Barr, Charles (1962) 'Some Other Aspects of Editing', *Scope*, 4, 5, 11 December, 16–21.

Bordwell, David & Kristin Thompson (1986) *Film Art*, Second Edition. New York: Alfred A. Knopf.

Burch, Noël (1969) *Praxis du cinéma*. Paris: Gallimard.

_____ (1973) *Theory of Film Practice*, Trans. Helen R. Lane. London: Secker and Warburg.

Carroll, Noël (1996) *Theorizing the Moving Image*. Cambridge: Cambridge University Press.

Dmytryk, Edward (1984) *On Film Editing*. London: Focal Press.

Fairservice, Don (2001) *Film Editing: History, Theory and Practice*. Manchester: Manchester University Press.

Godard, Jean-Luc (1968) 'Montage, mon beau souci', in Toby Mussman (ed.) *Jean-Luc Godard: A Critical Anthology*, Trans. Nell Cox. New York: E.P. Dutton, 47–9.

Henderson, Brian (1976) 'The Long Take', in Bill Nichols (ed.) *Movies an Methods: An Anthology*. Berkeley: University of California Press, 314–24.

Maillot, Pierre & Valérie Mouroux (eds) (1994) 'Les Conceptions du montage', *CinéMaction*, vol. 72.

Murch, Walter (1995) *In the Blink of an Eye: A Perspective on Film Editing*. Los Angeles: Silman-James Press.

Perkins, V.F. (1991) *Film as Film*. London: Penguin.

Reisz, Karel & Gavin Millar (1996) *The Technique of Film Editing*, Second edition. London: Focal Press.

Salt, Barry (1992) *Film Style and Technology: History and Analysis*. London: Starword.

Villain, Dominique (1991) *Le Montage au cinéma*. Paris: Cahiers du cinéma. Warren, Paul (1989) *Le Secret du star system américain: une stratégie du regard*. Montreal: Éditions de l'Hexagone.

SECONDARY READING

Amiel, Vincent (2001) *Esthétique du montage*. Paris: Nathan Cinéma.
Andrew, Dudley (ed.) (1987) *Breathless: Jean-Luc Godard, Director*. London: Rutgers University Press.
Anon. (1996) 'Interview with Thelma Schoonmaker', *Premiere* (US), 9:7, March, 42.
Assayas, Olivier & Serge Toubiana (1981) 'Profession: Monteuse', interview with Thelma Schoonmaker, *Cahiers du cinéma*, 321, March, iv.
Balázs, Béla (1970) *Theory of the Film: Character and Growth of a New Art*, Trans. Edith Bone. New York: Dover.
Balmuth, Bernard (1989) *Introduction to Film Editing*. Boston, Massachusetts and London: Focal Press.
Barthes, Roland (1970) *S/Z*. Paris: Seuil
Baudry, Jean-Louis (1970) 'Ideological Effects of the Basic Cinematographic Apparatus', in Patricia Rosen (ed.) (1986) *Narrative Apparatus, Ideology*. New York: Columbia University Press.
Bazin, André (1993) *Qu'est-ce que le cinéma?* Paris: Éditions du Cerf.
Bellour, Raymond (1980) 'Alterner/Raconter', in Raymond Bellour (ed.) *Le Cinéma américain: analyses de films*. Paris: Flammarion, 69–88.
Belton, John (1983) '*Under Capricorn*: Montage Entranced by Mise-en-scène', in *Cinema Stylists*. Metuchen, New Jersey: The Scarecrow Press, 39–58.
Berger, John (1972) *Ways of Seeing*. London: British Broadcasting Corporation and Harmondsworth/Penguin.
Bergstrom, Janet (1977) '*Jeanne Dielman, 23 Quai du Commerce, 1080 Bruxelles* by Chantal Akerman', *Camera Obscura*, 2, Fall, 114–21.
Bettetini, Gianfranco (1973) *The Language and Technique of the Film*. The Hague: Mouton.
Bobker, Lee R. (1969) 'Editing', in Lee R. Bobker (ed.) *Elements of Film*. New York: Harcourt Brace. 129–56.
Bogdanovich, Peter (1963) *The Cinema of Alfred Hitchcock*. New York: Museum of Modern Art Film Library.
_____ (1968) *John Ford*. Berkeley: University of California Press.
Bonitzer, Pascal (1981) '*Raging Bull* de Martin Scorsese: La solitude sans fond', *Cahiers du cinéma*, 321, March, 5–9.
Booth, Margaret (1938) 'The Cutter' in Stephen Watts (ed.) *Behind the Screen: How Films Are Made* London: Arthur Barker, 147–53.
Booth, Wayne (1961) *The Rhetoric of Fiction*. London: University of Chicago Press.
Borden, Lizzie (1995) '*Raging Bull*', *Sight and Sound*, 5, 2, 61.
Bordwell, David (1984) 'Jump Cuts and Blind Spots', *Wide Angle*, 6, 1, Spring, 4–11.
_____ (1985) *Narration in the Fiction Film*. London: Methuen.
_____ (1989) *Making Meaning: Inference and Rhetoric in the Interpretation of Cinema*. London: Harvard University Press.
_____ (1997) *On the History of Film Style*. Cambridge, Mass.: Harvard University Press.
Bordwell, David, Janet Staiger and Kristin Thompson (1985) *The Classical Hollywood Cinema*. London: Routledge.
Bouzereau, Laurent (1993) *The Alfred Hitchcock Quote Book*. New York: Citadel Press.
_____ (1994) *The Cutting Room Floor*. New York: Citadel Press.
Branigan, Edward (1975) 'Formal Permutations of the Point-of-View Shot', *Screen*, 16,

3, Autumn, 54–64.

_____ (1984) *Point of View in the Cinema: A Theory of Narration and Subjectivity in Classical Film*. Berlin: Mouton.

_____ (1992) *Narrative Comprehension and Film*. London: Routledge.

Branston, Brian (1967) *A Filmmaker's Guide to Planning, Directing and Shooting Films for Pleasure and Profit*. London: George Allen and Unwin.

Britton, Andrew (1991) 'Stars and Genre', in Christine Gledhill (ed.) *Stardom: The Industry of Desire*. London: Routledge, 198–206.

Brownlow, Kevin (1968) *The Parade's Gone By*. New York: Ballantine Books.

Butler, Jeremy G. (ed.) (1991) *Star Texts: Image and Performance in Film and Television*. Detroit: Wayne State University Press.

Butler, Alison (2002) *Women's Cinema: The Contested Screen*. London: Wallflower Press.

Cagle, Jess (1993), 'Many a slip...', *Empire*, 51, September, p. 96.

Cameron, Ian & V. F. Perkins (1963) 'Hitchcock', *Movie*, 6, January, 4–6.

Carroll, Noël (1978) 'Toward a Theory of Film Editing', *Millenium Film Journal*, 3, 79–99.

Champetier, Caroline (1978) 'Rencontre avec Chantal Akerman: *Les Rendez-vous d'Anna*', *Cahiers du cinéma*, 288, May, 52–61.

Ciment, Michel & Hubert Niogret (1992) ' A chacun sa couleur: entretien avec Quentin Tarantino', *Positif*, 379, September, 28–35.

Clifton, N. Roy (1983) *The Figure in Film*. London: Associated University Presses.

Collet, Jean (1962) 'L'Acteur à son insu dans les films de la Nouvelle Vague', in Claude Gauteur (ed.) *L'Acteur*. Paris: Études cinématographiques, 38–47.

Colpi, Henri, Jean-Luc Godard & André Bazin (1956) *Cahiers du cinéma*, 65, December, 26–36.

Cook, David (1996) *A History of Narrative Film*. London, New York: W.W. Norton. Third Edition.

Crawley, Tony (ed.) (1991) *Chambers Film Quotes*. Edinburgh: W.R. Chambers.

Crisp, Mike (1996) *The Practical Director*. Oxford: Focal Press.

Crittenden, Roger (1981) *Film Editing*. London: Thames and Hudson.

_____ (2001) 'All My Eye and Aristotle: Editing European Films', *Vertigo*, 2, 1, Spring, 3–5.

Dancyger, Ken (1993) *The Technique of Film and Video Editing*. Boston and London: Focal Press.

Dixon, Wheeler Winston (1997) *The Films of Jean-Luc Godard*. New York: State University of New York Press.

Doane, Mary Ann (1985) 'Ideology and the Practice of Sound Editing and Mixing', in Elizabeth Weis & John Belton (eds) *Film Sound: Theory and Practice*. New York: Columbia University Press, 54–62.

Douin, Jean-Luc (1994) *Jean-Luc Godard*. Paris: Rivages/Cinéma.

Dyer, Richard (1979) *Stars*. London: BFI.

Ebert, Roger & Gene Siskel (1991) *The Future of the Movies: Interviews with Scorsese, Spielberg and Lucas*. Kansas: Andrews and McMeel.

Eisenstein, Sergei (1949) *Film Form*. New York: Harcourt Brace.

Ellis, Jack C. (1995) *A History of Film*, Fourth Edition. London: Allyn and Bacon.

Ellis, John (1992) *Visible Fictions: Cinema, Television, Video*. London: Routledge.

Faller, Greg S. (1997) 'Thelma Schoonmaker', in Grace Jeromski (ed.) *International*

*Dictionary of Films and Filmmakers: Writers and Production Artists.* London: St James Press, 746–7.

French, Philip (ed.) (1993) *Malle on Malle.* London: Faber and Faber.

Gardies, André & Jean Bessalel (1995) *Deux cents mots-clés de la théorie du cinéma.* Paris: Éditions du Cerf.

Gauteur, Claude (ed.) (1962) *L'Acteur.* Paris: Études cinématographiques.

Giannetti, Louis (1996) *Understanding Movies.* New Jersey: Prentice Hall, Chapter: 'Editing' , 129–96.

Giannetti, Louis & Scott Eyman (1996) *Flashback: A Brief History of Film.* Third Edition. Englewood Cliffs, New Jersey: Prentice Hall.

Gibbs, John (2001) *Mise-en-scène: Film Style and Interpretation.* London: Wallflower Press.

Gledhill, Christine (ed.) (1991) *Stardom: The Industry of Desire.* London: Routledge.

Godard, Jean-Luc (1980) *Introduction à une véritable histoire du cinéma.* Paris: Albatros.

\_\_\_\_ (1989) 'Défense et illustration du découpage classique', in *Godard par Godard: les années 'Cahiers'.* Paris: Flammarion, 58–64.

Gottlieb, Sidney (ed.) (1995) *Hitchcock on Hitchcock.* London: Faber and Faber, 253–61.

Graham, Peter (ed.) (1968) *The New Wave.* London: Secker and Warburg.

Hargreaves, Robert (1993) 'Bad Cuts Are Sexy', *Vertigo*, 1, 1, Spring, 46–7.

Harrington, John (1973) *The Rhetoric of Film.* London: Holt, Rinehart and Winston.

Hill, John & Pamela Church Gibson (eds) (1998) *The Oxford Guide to Film Studies.* Oxford: Oxford University Press.

Hillier, Jim & Peter Wollen (eds) (1996) *Howard Hawks: American Artist.* London: BFI.

Huss, Roy & Norman Silverstein (1968) *Film Experience: Elements of Motion Picture Art.* New York: Harper and Row.

Jacobs, Lewis (1939) 'Art: Edwin S. Porter and the Editing Principles', in Lewis Jacobs (ed.) *The Rise of the American Film.* New York: Harcourt and Brace, 35–51.

Jayamanne, Laleen (1980) 'Modes of Performance in Chantal Akerman's *Jeanne Dielman, 23 Quai du Commerce, 1080 Bruxelles*', *Australian Journal of Screen Theory*, 8, July, 97–111.

Jousse, Thierry & Frédéric Strauss (1991) 'Entretien avec Agnès Guillemot', *Cahiers du cinéma*, special issue on Godard, 10 August, 60–3.

Kelly, Mary Pat (1980) *Martin Scorsese: The First Decade.* Pleasantville, New York: Redgrave.

\_\_\_\_ (1991) *Martin Scorsese: A Journey.* New York: Thunder's Mouth Press.

Kepley, Vance Jnr. (1983) 'Spatial Articulation in the Classical Cinema: A Scene from *His Girl Friday*', *Wide Angle*, 5, 3, 50–8.

King, Barry (1991) 'Articulating Stardom', in Jeremy G. Butler (ed.), *Star Texts: Image and Performance in Film and Television.* Detroit: Wayne State University Press, 125–54.

Knight, Arthur (1959) 'Editing: The Lost Art', *Films and Filming*, 5, 9, June, 12, 33.

Kobal, John (1972) 'The Time, the Place and the Girl', *Focus on Film*, Summer, 15–29.

Kolker, Robert Philip (1980) *A Cinema of Loneliness: Penn, Kubrick, Coppola, Scorsese, Altman.* Oxford: Oxford University Press.

Konigsberg, Ira (1987) *The Complete Film Dictionary.* London: Bloomsbury.

Lanham, Richard A. (1991) *A Handbook of Rhetorical Figures*, Second Edition. Berkeley: University of California Press.

La Valley, Albert J. (ed.) (1972) *Focus on Hitchcock*. Englewood Cliffs, New Jersey: Prentice-Hall.

Lesage, Julia (1976) *The Films of Jean-Luc Godard and Their Use of Brechtian Drama*. Ann Arbor: University Microfilms.

Levaco, Ronald (ed. and trans.) (1974) *Kuleshov on Film: Writings by Lev Kuleshov*. Berkeley: University of California Press.

Loader, Jayne (1977) '*Jeanne Dielman*: Death in Instalments', *Jump Cut*, 16, November, 10–12.

Lo Brutto, Vincent (1991) *Selected Takes: Film Editors on Editing*. Westport, Connecticut: Praeger.

Malden, Karl (1997) *When Do I Start?* New York: Simon and Schuster.

McGrath, Declan (2001) *Editing and Post-production*. Crans-Près-Céligny: Rotovision.

Marie, Michel (1990) '"It really makes you sick!": Jean-Luc Godard's *A bout de souffle*', in Susan Hayward & Ginette Vincendeau (eds) *French Film: Texts and Contexts*. London: Routledge, 201–15.

Mast, Gerald (1986) *A Short History of the Movies*, Fourth Edition. London: Collier Macmillan.

Metz, Christian (1972) 'Ponctuations et démarcations dans le film de diégèse', *Essais sur la signification au cinéma*, Vol. 2. Paris: Klincksieck, 111–37.

_____ (1974) *Film Language: A Semiotics of the Cinema*. Trans. Michael Taylor. New York: Oxford University Press.

Milne, Tom (ed.) (1972) *Godard on Godard*. New York: Viking.

Mitry, Jean (1957) *S.M. Eisenstein*. Brussels: Club du Livre du Cinéma. Chapter: 'Le "montage d'attractions" et les théories du montage', 42–76.

_____ (1983) 'Montage et non-montage', *Cinématographe*, 86, February, 70–3.

Modleski, Tania (1988) *The Women Who Knew Too Much: Hitchcock and Feminist Theory*. New York: Methuen.

Monaco, James (1974) *The Films of Jean-Luc Godard*. New York: New School Film Department.

_____ (1981) *How to Read a Film*. Oxford: Oxford University Press.

Mulvey, Laura (1975) 'Visual Pleasure and Narrative Cinema', *Screen*, 16, 3, Autumn, 6–18.

Mussman, Toby (ed.) (1968) *Jean-Luc Godard*. New York: E.P. Dutton.

Nichols, Bill (ed.) (1976) *Movies and Methods: An Anthology*. Berkeley: University of California Press.

Nowell-Smith, Geoffrey (1996) *Oxford History of World Cinema*. Oxford: Oxford University Press.

Ohanian Thomas, A. (1993) *Digital Non-Linear Editing: New Approaches to Editing Film and Video*. London: Focal Press.

Oldham, Gabriella (1992) *First Cut: Conversations with Film Editors*. Berkeley: University of California Press.

Orr, John (1993) *Cinema and Modernity*. Cambridge: Polity Press.

Perlmutter, Ruth (1979) 'Feminine Absence: A Political Aesthetic in Chantal Akerman's *Jeanne Dielman, 23 Quai du Commerce, 1080 Bruxelles*', *Quarterly Review of Film Studies*, 4, 2, Spring, 125–33.

Plantinga, Carl L. (1997) *Rhetoric and Representation in Nonfiction Film*. Cambridge University Press.

'Prime Cut: Seventy-five Editors' Filmographies and Supporting Material' (1977) *Film*

*Comment*, 13, 2, March-April, 6–23; 26–9.

Price, James (1965) 'A Film is a Film: Some Notes on Jean-Luc Godard', *Evergreen Review* 9: 38, November, 46–53.

Pudovkin, V.I. (1933) *Film Technique*. London: George Newnes.

Ricœur, Paul (1978) *The Rule of Metaphor*. Trans. Robert Czerny. London: Routledge and Kegan Paul.

Rosen, Philip (ed.) (1986) *Narrative, Apparatus, Ideology*. New York: Columbia University Press.

Rosenblum, Ralph (1979) *When the Shooting Stops, the Cutting Begins: A Film Editor's Story*. New York: Penguin.

Sarris, Andrew (1964) 'Waiting for Godard', in Toby Mussman (ed.) (1968) *Jean-Luc Godard: A Critical Anthology*. New York: E.P. Dutton, 131–6.

Schiff, Stephen (1996) 'The *Casino* Cut: What Does It Take to Make a Great Film?', *The Independent on Sunday*, 4 February, 16.

Sharff, Stefan (1997) *The Art of Looking in Hitchcock's Rear Window*. New York: Limelight Editions.

Sherwood, Rick (1991) 'In Rhythm with Martin Scorsese: Editor Thelma Schoonmaker from *Woodstock* to *Goodfellas*', *Hollywood Reporter*, 316, 12, 11 February, S8–S9.

Simon, William (1979) 'An Approach to Point of View', *Film Reader*, 4, 145–50.

Singer, Ben (1989/90) '*Jeanne Dielman*: Cinematic Interrogation and "Amplification"', *Millenium Film Journal*, 22, Winter/Spring, 56–75.

Smith, Murray (1995) *Engaging Characters: Fiction, Emotion and the Cinema*. Oxford: Clarendon Press.

Sontag, Susan (1968) 'Going to the Movies: Godard', *The Partisan Review*, 2, Spring, 210–313.

Spottiswoode, Raymond (1935) *A Grammar of the Film*. London: Faber.

Stacey, Jackie (1994) *Star Gazing: Hollywood Cinema and Female Spectatorship*. London: Routledge.

Stam, Robert & Roberta Pearson (1983) 'Hitchcock's *Rear Window*: Reflexivity and the Critique of Voyeurism', *Enclitic*, 7, 1, Spring, 136–45.

Taylor, John Russell (1973) *Directors and Directions*. New York: Hill and Wang.

\_\_\_\_ (1978) *Hitch: The Life and Work of Alfred Hitchcock*. London: Abacus.

Thomas, Deborah (2000) *Reading Hollywood: Spaces and Meanings in American Film*. London: Wallflower Press.

Thompson, Kristin (1999) *Storytelling in the New Hollywood: Understanding Classical Narrative Technique*. Cambridge, Mass.: Harvard University Press.

Thompson, Roy (1993) *Grammar of the Edit*. London: Focal Press.

Thomson, David (1989) 'The Lives of Supporting Players', *Film Comment*, 25, 6, November–December, 32–57.

Thomson, David & Ian Christie (eds) (1996) *Scorsese on Scorsese*. London: Faber and Faber.

Truffaut, François (1954) 'Une certaine tendance du cinéma français', *Cahiers du Cinéma*, 6, 31, January, 15–29.

\_\_\_\_ (1962) Interview, *Cahiers du Cinéma*, 138, December, 40–59.

\_\_\_\_ (1986) *Hitchcock*. London: Paladin. Revised edition.

*Variety* (1960) Review of *A bout de souffle*, 27 January, 6.

Vincendeau, Ginette (1992) 'The Exception and the Rule', *Sight and Sound*, 2, 8, December, 34–6.

_____ (1998) 'The Indiscreet Charm of Jeanne Moreau', *Sight and Sound*, 8, 12, December, 32–5.

Watts, Stephen (ed.) (1938) *Behind the Screen: How Films Are Made*. London: Arthur Barker.

Weis, Elizabeth & John Belton (eds) (1985) *Film Sound: Theory and Practice*. New York: Columbia University Press.

Wood, Robin (1989) *Hitchcock's Films Revisited*. London: Faber and Faber.

Learning Resources
Centre